Conspiracy Theories and the Nordic Countries

This book explores the relevance of conspiracy theories in the modern social and political history of the Nordic countries.

The Nordic countries have traditionally imagined themselves as stable, wealthy, egalitarian welfare states. Conspiracy theories, mistrust, and disunity, the argument goes, happened elsewhere in Europe (especially Eastern Europe), the Middle East, or in the United States. This book paints a different picture by demonstrating that conspiracy theories have always existed in the Nordic region, both as a result of structural tensions between different groups and in the aftermath of traumatic events, but seem to have become more prominent over the last 30 or 40 years. While the book covers events and developments in each of the Nordic countries (Sweden, Norway, Denmark, Iceland, and Finland), it is not a comparative country analysis. Rather, the book focuses on conspiracy theories in and about the Nordic region *as a region*, arguing that similarities in the trajectories of conspiratorial thinking are interesting to examine in cultural, social, and political terms. The book takes a thematic approach, including looking at states and elites; family, gender and sexuality; migration and the outside view on the Nordic region; conspiracy theories about the Nordic countries; and Nordic noir.

This book will be of great interest to researchers on extremism, conspiracy theories, and the politics of the Nordic countries.

Anastasiya Astapova is Senior Research Fellow in the Department of Estonian and Comparative Folklore at the University of Tartu, Estonia.

Eirikur Bergmann is Professor of Politics at Bifrost University, Iceland.

Asbjørn Dyrendal is Professor of Religious Studies at the Norwegian University of Science and Technology in Trondheim.

Annika Rabo is Professor Emeritus of Social Anthropology at Stockholm University, Sweden.

Kasper Grotle Rasmussen is Associate Professor of American History at the University of Southern Denmark.

Hulda Thórisdóttir is Associate Professor of Political Science at the University of Iceland.

Andreas Önnerfors is Professor of the History of Sciences and Ideas at the University of Gothenburg, Sweden.

Conspiracy Theories
Series Editors: Peter Knight, University of Manchester,
and **Michael Butter,** University of Tübingen

Conspiracy theories have a long history and exist in all modern societies. However, their visibility and significance are increasing today. Conspiracy theories can no longer be simply dismissed as the product of a pathological mindset located on the political margins.

This series provides a nuanced and scholarly approach to this most contentious of subjects. It draws on a range of disciplinary perspectives including political science, sociology, history, media and cultural studies, area studies and behavioural sciences. Issues covered include the psychology of conspiracy theories, changes in conspiratorial thinking over time, the role of the Internet, regional and political variations and the social and political impact of conspiracy theories.

The series will include edited collections, single-authored monographs and short-form books.

Strategic Conspiracy Narratives
A Semiotic Approach
Mari-Liis Madisson and Andreas Ventsel

Conspiracy Narratives South of the Border
Bad Hombres Do the Twist
Gonzalo Soltero

Conspiracy Theories in Eastern Europe
Tropes and Trends
Edited by Anastasiya Astapova, Onoriu Colăcel, Corneliu Pintilescu and Tamás Scheibner

Conspiracy Theories and the Nordic Countries
Anastasiya Astapova, Eirikur Bergmann, Asbjørn Dyrendal, Annika Rabo, Kasper Grotle Rasmussen, Hulda Thórisdóttir, Andreas Önnerfors

Conspiracy Theories and the Nordic Countries

Anastasiya Astapova,
Eirikur Bergmann, Asbjørn Dyrendal,
Annika Rabo, Kasper Grotle
Rasmussen, Hulda Thórisdóttir and
Andreas Önnerfors

LONDON AND NEW YORK

First published 2021
by Routledge
2 Park Square, Milton Park, Abingdon, Oxon OX14 4RN

and by Routledge
52 Vanderbilt Avenue, New York, NY 10017

Routledge is an imprint of the Taylor & Francis Group, an informa business

© 2021 Anastasiya Astapova, Eirikur Bergmann, Asbjørn Dyrendal,
Annika Rabo, Kasper Grotle Rasmussen, Hulda Thórisdóttir,
Andreas Önnerfors

The right of Anastasiya Astapova, Eirikur Bergmann, Asbjørn Dyrendal,
Annika Rabo, Kasper Grotle Rasmussen, Hulda Thórisdóttir, Andreas Önnerfors
to be identified as authors of this work has been asserted by them in
accordance with sections 77 and 78 of the Copyright, Designs and Patents Act 1988.

All rights reserved. No part of this book may be reprinted or reproduced or utilised
in any form or by any electronic, mechanical, or other means, now known or
hereafter invented, including photocopying and recording, or in any information
storage or retrieval system, without permission in writing from the publishers.

Trademark notice: Product or corporate names may be trademarks or registered trademarks,
and are used only for identification and explanation without intent to infringe.

British Library Cataloguing-in-Publication Data
A catalogue record for this book is available from the British Library

Library of Congress Cataloging-in-Publication Data
Names: Astapova, Anastasiya, author. Title: Conspiracy theories and
the Nordic countries / Anastasiya Astapova, [and six others].
Description: Milton Park, Abingdon, Oxon;
New York, NY: Routledge, 2021. | Series: Conspiracy theories |
Includes bibliographical references and index.
Identifiers: LCCN 2020037498 (print) | LCCN 2020037499 (ebook) |
ISBN 9780367354473 (hardback) | ISBN 9780367822491 (ebook)
Subjects: LCSH: Conspiracy theories–Scandinavia. |
Political culture–Scandinavia. | Radicalism–Scandinavia.
Classification: LCC HV6295.S34 A88 2021 (print) |
LCC HV6295.S34 (ebook) | DDC 001.9/80948–dc23
LC record available at https://lccn.loc.gov/2020037498
LC ebook record available at https://lccn.loc.gov/2020037499

ISBN: 978-0-367-35447-3 (hbk)
ISBN: 978-0-367-82249-1 (ebk)

Typeset in Times New Roman
by Newgen Publishing UK

Contents

	Preface	vii
1	Conspiracy theories and the Nordic countries	1
2	The state and secret elites in the Nordic countries	15
3	Family, gender, and sexuality	33
4	Migration and the dangerous outsiders: anti-immigrant conspiracy theories in the Nordic countries	53
5	Conspiracy theories about the Nordic countries	73
6	Nordic noir	89
	Bibliography	105
	Index	121

Preface

The image that the Nordics project around the world is often one of benign and prosperous welfare states. Peaceful, but boring. Affluent areas where not much noteworthy happens. The authors of this book all belonged to the network *Comparative Analysis of Conspiracy Theories in Europe* (COMPACT), funded by the European Cooperation for Science and Technology (COST). When we met in 2016, we could feel that the focus of our collaborators was not on the Nordics. Not at all. When talking about conspiracy theories, their gaze turned rather to America, to Eastern Europe, towards the south, but the Nordics were not of much interest to them. Not yet. We, however, knew that the area was much more interesting than might meet the eye at first glance. As William Shakespeare wrote, there might indeed something be rotten in the state of Denmark – and in the other Nordic countries as well.

It was during a network meeting at the Bilderberg Hotel in the Netherlands in May 2018, the site of one of the most influential contemporary conspiracy theories, that we first started to contemplate writing this book. We understood that our other European and American colleagues had not been exposed to much literature on conspiracy theories in the Nordic countries. We indeed realized that there wasn't actually much of a literature attempting to make sense of conspiracy theories in or of the region. This book is an attempt to fill some of that gap.

We are a group of seven scholars, citizens or residents of Denmark, Estonia, Iceland, Norway, and Sweden. We hail from different disciplines, folklore, history, history of science and ideas, political science, religious studies, social anthropology, and social psychology. It is our hope that this dynamic can put us in a favourable position to examine both the meaning and the impact of conspiracy theories in and of the Nordic countries.

viii *Preface*

Initially, we were mainly intrigued by tales of clandestine elites in the Nordics, secretly plotting against the interest and welfare of the common people. Soon, however, we realized that the conspiratorial field in the Nordics was and is much more abundant. Still, we make no claim of covering the field in its entirety. Instead, we see this short book as only a first attempt to place the Nordics within the larger scene of conspiracy theories studies.

We are indebted to a great many people and institutions. First of all, we want to thank the leaders of the network that brought us together, Professors Michael Butter and Peter Knight. We also want to thank all our other greatly supportive colleagues in the network who helped shape this book through intriguing discussions. We owe thanks to many others. We thank Véronique Campion-Vincent for valuable comments, Laima Vaigė for ideas, and Eliot Borenstein for the generous sharing of material from a pre-published version *Plots Against Russia*. Author Ivo de Figuirero, Terje Emberland at the Center for Research on Holocaust and Religious Minorities in Oslo, and Kjetil Braut Simonsen at the Jewish Museum in Oslo, gave tips on and copies of some relevant sources on far right and anti-Semitic sources from different periods. Simonsen also gave feedback on an early version of chapter three. Titus Hjelm at Helsinki University had his brains picked for Finnish cases. Christine Myrvang at BI Norwegian Business School in Oslo helped with some ideas on gender and conspiracy theories in the interwar period, and Andrew Mitchell at Stockholm University corrected some details on Nordic fears of wolves. A part of this research was supported by personal research funding from the Estonian Research Council PSG48: 'Performative Negotiations of Belonging in Contemporary Estonia'. We finally want to thank Lindsay Porter for proofreading the manuscript.

June 2020 – Anastasiya, Andreas, Asbjørn, Annika, Eirikur, Hulda, Kasper

1 Conspiracy theories and the Nordic countries

In recent years the Nordics have garnered fascination far beyond their borders for gory murders, rape, corruption, and conspiracies – although invented by writers of the *Nordic noir* genre. Following the incredible success of Stieg Larsson's crime novels, the *Millennium* trilogy in the mid-2000s, Nordic noir was propelled to international fame. Novels and TV shows depicting peaceful Nordic societies beset by crimes and conspiracies clearly had an irresistible allure for large swathes of audiences from the United States to Australia.

It might seem contradictory that countries known for their peacefulness, prosperity, and low crime rate could produce such an abundance of chilling crime novels. Some have suggested that the origins of Nordic noir can be traced to one of the most traumatic events in Sweden's modern history – the murder of the country's Prime Minister Olof Palme in 1986. Along with his wife, Palme was walking home late at night from a movie theatre in central Stockholm when an assassin suddenly appeared and fatally shot him in the back at close range. The murderer escaped and remained at large.

Although the murder was traumatizing, its aftermath, a botched investigation that was still ongoing more than three decades later, is claimed to have impacted Swedes more than the murder itself (West-Knights 2019). More than 10,000 people have been questioned in relation to the murder, and the material takes up 250 metres of shelf space in police storage. The unsolved murder caused even greater trauma in Sweden than the killing of President John F. Kennedy (JFK) did in the United States (Åsard 2006). The term "Palmessjukdom," or Palme sickness, is used to describe obsession with the murder, covering everything from the 130 individuals who have confessed to the murder to the countless numbers of amateur investigators who have poured their hearts into trying to solve the crime. The perceived incompetence of the authorities in solving the case affected political trust and caused

2 *Conspiracy theories and Nordic countries*

damage to democracy, while, as recently as 2016, the Swedish prime minister described the unsolved murder as 'an open wound in Swedish society' (in Bbc.com 2018).

Theories about who was behind the murder are abundant and range from disgruntled lone wolves to undercover operations by foreign governments. Olof Palme spearheaded many of the left-leaning social policies Sweden has become known for and he was not shy of taking a strong stance on international issues of the era, such as on apartheid in South Africa. Because of his somewhat radical reforms and non-compromising political style, he faced strong opponents among the public and politicians, both domestically and internationally. Lennart Gustafsson, an investigator on the case from 1986 to 2016, said in an interview that 'you could suspect half the Swedish population' (Johnson 2012).

The Swedish novelist Henning Mankell, often considered the father of Nordic noir, was highly influenced by the case. The journalist and crime writer Stieg Larsson developed a deep interest in the unsolved murder starting when he was a young investigative journalist. By the time of his untimely death from a heart attack in 2004, he had amassed twenty cardboard boxes worth of material on the murder and was working on a book about it, suggesting that South African security and intelligence services were behind the murder via a far-right Swedish mercenary (West-Knights 2019).

Other traumatic events have also spawned (or even been spawned by) conspiracy theories. The sinking of the ferry MS *Estonia* in 1994 resulted in 852 casualties, the largest loss of human life in European waters during peacetime. The ferry was crossing the Baltic sea from Tallinn, Estonia, to Stockholm, Sweden, on a September night. The weather wasn't good and an official investigation concluded that the bow door of the ferry had opened due to the strong waves, which resulted in the ship flooding with water. This fairly straightforward conclusion did not prevent alternative theories from gaining some traction. Most notably, a conspiracy theory put forward by a German journalist was that the ferry had been transporting sensitive military equipment, and that what caused the sinking was a deliberate explosion that Swedish, Russian, and British authorities were eager to conceal (Davis 2005).

Of a very different nature was the financial crisis that hit Iceland in 2009, when the three national banks could not finance their debts and collapsed, leaving the Icelandic economy reeling on the edge of bankruptcy. The loss was significant for both ordinary depositors in Iceland as well as large international financial institutions which had extended loans to Icelandic businessmen and companies. Although the dominant

Conspiracy theories and Nordic countries   3

view was that the crisis was the result of reckless business practices, a vocal minority claims that British and American banks, entangled with their authorities, deliberately decided to let Iceland crash as a warning to other countries. Later, during the aftermath and slow recovery from the crisis, Sigmundur Gunnlaugsson, the former prime minister of Iceland, had to resign due to not being transparent about how his wife had invested large sums of her substantial personal wealth in off-shore accounts. During this political scandal, Gunnlaugsson and his supporters accused foreign creditors of using secret surveillance and intimidation on him and other high-profile government officials.

Conspiracy beliefs are forms of *theodicy*, that is, they are explanations of evil events and difficult circumstances. As such, they compete with other explanations of evil, and their success varies. Conspiracy theories have always existed in the Nordic countries, though perhaps in a quieter fashion and less focused on the evils of the state than has been seen in many other places. In the last roughly 50 years, however, conspiracy theories seem to have an increased public presence in the Nordic countries. Three overall reasons suggest this may be true. First, while social and political trust remain high in the Nordic countries, there has been a rising, minority 'cultural backlash' (Norris and Inglehart 2019) against the rapid cultural change towards socially libertarian attitudes, increasing the level of populist and authoritarian responses. Second, and particularly tied to this, migration to the Nordic countries and popular reaction to it have further challenged societal cohesion and sparked suspicion and conspiratorial ideas. Third, the high level of education and language proficiency, with English as the main foreign language, has made conspiracy narratives highly available. The strong transatlantic influence – especially evident since the turn of the millennium – of conspiracy theories against the state and the elites, has played a role in not merely bringing in new conspiracy theories, but in making conspiracy theorizing salient as a central mode of explaining evil. Conversely, globalization and the welfare success of the Nordic countries has also made them famous around the world, not least as protagonists of conspiracy theories.

The field of study of conspiracy theories in the Nordic countries has been underdeveloped. With this book we aim to partially fill the gap by providing a general overview of the topic and discussing some examples of conspiratorialism in the region. We will be drawing out several case studies, both from specific countries and from the region as a whole. Some of the cases illustrate particular dynamics, while others have been especially important to public discourse and/or politics. Both types provide a broader picture of the state of conspiracy theories,

4 *Conspiracy theories and Nordic countries*

their history, meanings, and, to some degree, importance in the Nordic countries. While the focus here is on the Nordics, the book draws out some comparative perspectives, showing how cultural diffusion of international conspiracy narratives changes them to suit new circumstances. The Nordic self-perception may long have been that 'conspiracy theories' belong to the irrational other; we show how they have been made relevant for and adapted to Nordic culture. Moreover, the dynamics in which they have been made, has partially made conspiracy theories *about* the Nordic countries salient also abroad, especially in Russia, the nearby Baltic countries and Eastern Europe.

What is a conspiracy theory?

The term 'conspiracy theory' is applied in various ways. The broad definition of political scientists Uscinski and Parent (2014: 32) is useful here: 'an explanation of historical, ongoing, or future events that cites as a main causal factor a small group of powerful persons [...] acting in secret for their own benefit against the common good'. A host of problems often associated with conspiracy theories could be added, mostly regarding epistemically questionable, immunizing strategies to avoid falsification, but also demands about the degree of elaboration ('theory') involved (e.g. Butter 2014). In this book, 'conspiracy theory' is most often used as the vernacular form that covers the gamut from conspiracy rumours to elaborate theories. The implication is that while actual conspiracies are abundant, 'conspiracy theories' are epistemically suspect, but still serve other, sometimes vital, social purposes. They typically, as mentioned above, explain 'evil' in terms of hidden human agency (Barkun 2003), and in that regard, they often express arenas of social conflict, but distort facts and deflect blame (Butter 2014). Combined, this covers how we use 'conspiracy theory' in this book.

A 'conspiracy belief' is, then, when an individual assumes that a conspiracy theory provides an acceptable approximation of an explanation of particular events. Some have found it useful to distinguish the endorsement of specific conspiracy theories from a more general dispositional propensity for belief in conspiracies. Imhoff and Bruder (2014) labelled this tendency 'conspiracy mentality' and argued that it functions as a generalized political attitude in itself. Conspiracy thinking, however, should not be seen as a sign of personal illness, but rather as a way of dealing with the complexity of the modern world. The conspiracy theory is therefore often a symptom of a perceived imbalance between the powerful and those subjected to their rule (cf. Knight 2002: 7).

Conspiracy theories and Nordic countries 5

The level of conspiracy beliefs tends to increase when levels of social trust fall and when scores on democracy and human development are low. This is part of what makes the Nordic countries an interesting case.

The Nordics – a snapshot of a region

The five Nordic states (Denmark, Finland, Iceland, Norway, Sweden) and the three self-rule territories of the area (Åland Islands, Greenland, Faroe Islands) represent a clearly distinguishable geopolitical entity in northern Europe. Integrationist efforts that led to the unification of, for example, Italy or Germany failed in the Nordic region in the nineteenth century, giving birth instead to the Nordic system of independent nation states. While keeping to their differences as independent nation states, the Nordic five share many similarities. All are relatively small states, though Iceland borders the micro-state category and Sweden is close to being considered midsize. The Nordics share a history and cultural heritage influenced first by pagan mythology and later by Christianity. Lutheran state churches are still strong throughout the region and, ethnically, most of the population is of Nordic descent.

The political culture of the region is furthermore easily distinguishable as coordinated market economies within boundaries of democratic welfare nation states, based on gender equality, nature protection, and rigorous bureaucratic regulations. The public sector in the Nordics ranks amongst the largest in the Western world. Highly redistributive wide-ranging welfare-oriented public services are supported by relatively high taxes, leading to a relatively narrow – albeit increasing – income gap in the global context. Trust in collective institutions is high, and democratic traditions are strong.

The international image of the Nordics as trusting, peaceful, and prosperous is not entirely without merit as the Nordic countries are usually found towards the top of international economic, social, and other social progress indices. This is clearly gleaned from Table 1.1, which shows the ranking of the Nordic countries on four such international indicators: *Human Development Index*, which gauges life expectancy, educational attainment, and gross domestic product per capita; *Global Gender Gap*, which measures the economic participation and opportunity, educational attainment, health and survival, and political empowerment of women; *Democracy Index*, which consists of the five subcategories, electoral process and pluralism, civil liberties, functioning of government, political participation, and political culture; and finally, *Global Peace Index*, which consists of ten categories that assess safety and security in a country.

6 *Conspiracy theories and Nordic countries*

Table 1.1 Ranking of the Nordic countries on four international social progress indices

Social Progress Index	HDI	GGG	DI	GPI
Year	2018	2018	2018	2019
Denmark	11	13	4	5
Finland	15	4	6	14
Iceland	6	1	2	1
Norway	1	2	1	20[a]
Sweden	7	3	3	3

a Norway's relatively poor ranking on the peace index stems from the high military expenditure as a percentage of GDP.

HDI: Human Development Index; **GGG**: Global Gender Gap; **DI**: Democracy Index; **GPI**: Global Peace Index.

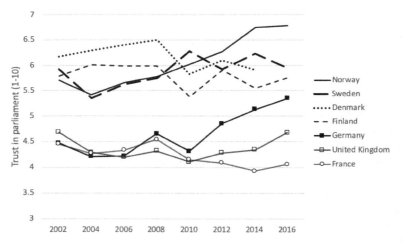

Figure 1.1 Average trust in the national parliament for seven different countries from 2002 to 2016, according to results from the European Social Survey.

Figure 1.1 uses data from the European Social Survey (European Social Survey, 2018) to show how trust in parliament has remained fairly stable with only temporary fluctuations in the Nordic countries from 2002 until 2016 (Iceland is missing because of sporadic participation in the ESS). The figure also shows that trust in parliament is consistently higher in the Nordics than trust in the three comparison countries: Germany, the United Kingdom, and France.

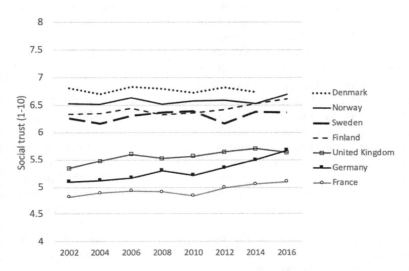

Figure 1.2 Social trust for seven different countries from 2002 to 2016, according to results from the European Social Survey using three survey items.

A non-political, more general tendency to trust is reflected in a measure of social trust, an index composed of how people rate the following three statements: 'Most people can be trusted or you can't be too careful', 'most of the time people helpful or mostly looking out for themselves', and 'most people try to take advantage of you, or try to be fair'. As can be seen in Figure 1.2, again the pattern to emerge is that of stability over time and clearly higher than the social trust in France, Germany, and the United Kingdom, although the latter two countries have seen an increase in social trust over time. It is worth emphasizing that the ESS measures *expressed* trust by respondents, which makes cross-country comparison complicated. It may be, for example, that people in the Nordics are generally more reluctant to express negative attitudes about their society compared to respondents in other countries.

Furthermore, the internal political discourse on the Nordics is generally positive. With political integrationist Scandinavianism[1] already being abandoned in the wake of the Napoleonic wars, cultural Nordism developed in conjunction with the nation states and was in fact seen to complement their respective nationhood creations.

The Nordics were never champions of European integration, which started only long after the system of Nordic nation states was already

8 *Conspiracy theories and Nordic countries*

well rooted. Iceland and Norway, for example, remain outside the European Union (EU), although they are members of the European Economic Area. Additionally, Sweden and Finland are non-members of NATO, to which all other Nordic states (as well as many EU members) belong. Rather, the Nordics can all be categorized as active but somewhat reluctant participants in the European project. Contrary to the idea of Europe, which often is seen to threaten the idea of the nation, Norden is seen as a relatively benign political idea. It is a cultural political project, situated between nation and Europe. The Norden concept holds strong collective connotations, but it stops short of supranational political integration. To fully comprehend Nordic politics, one has to examine the triangular relationship and the tension between 'Nation', 'Norden' and 'Europe'. In some regards, Norden functions as intermediary between the national and the European level (see Hansen, 2003: 12). Though the concept of Norden is interwoven in the discourse on Europe, it is, at least in the more prominent debate, still, rarely positioned as a credible alternative to Europe. For that, European integration in the region has gone too far.

The Nordic political culture of intra-inclusiveness, however, also has an external side of exclusion, often leading to intolerance against the foreign and sometimes to outright xenophobia. With the influx of immigrants starting in the 1960s and 1970s, this has at times led to troubled race relations and conspiracy theories about outsiders in the Nordic countries. Periods of economic downturn, especially following the oil crises in the 1970s and the financial crash in the 2000s, have further exacerbated this trend of suspicion against immigrants and refugees as 'welfare tourists'. These views, which will be explored further in Chapter 4, also continue to resonate with other European countries, most notably France, Italy, Germany, Hungary, and Poland, and the influence probably goes both ways.

Conspiracy theories about the elite collusion with catastrophic effects on the general population have also become more common – especially in the new millennium. Trust in the monied interests and the entire banking sector dropped as a result of the 2008 financial crisis and more recent money laundering scandals in both Denmark and Sweden (Ahlander, Vaish, and O'Donnel, 2019). Furthermore, the state became a central culprit following various Nordic countries' participation in the war on terror. The war was fought and continues to be fought in theatres all over the world, and the loss of Nordic life in these operations became the foundational motive for the spread of 9/11-related conspiracy theories.

Conspiracy theories in the Nordics – by the numbers

Conspiracy theories travel. In recent decades, they have often travelled from the United States to other regions, by routes influenced by globalization processes. As mentioned above, the Nordic countries typically favour English as a second language, which facilitates consumption of American narratives. Through popular culture, news media, and imported products, American influence has remained high in the Nordic countries since at least the Second World War. Major American traumatic events, such as the Kennedy assassination and 9/11, have impacted the lives of people in the Nordic countries because of shared cultural values and because of interconnected foreign policies. Can we see this influence also in the prevalence of beliefs in conspiracy theories in the Nordics? Have Nordic citizens embraced international conspiracy theories as enthusiastically as Americans, for example? What about local conspiracy theories?

Reliable cross-country comparison of the prevalence of conspiracy beliefs in the different Nordic countries is as of yet impossible because no coordinated survey data exists from all the countries. We know from the extant research (e.g. Smallpage et al. 2020) that answers people give about their belief in specific conspiracy theories depend heavily on question wording. As a result, comparison between surveys should be approached very carefully, even between questions that seem almost identical.

The conspiracy theory that the 9/11 attacks were an inside job by individuals within the US government is accepted by around 19% of Americans, according to a study by Oliver and Wood (2014), and around 53% of Americans agree with the much milder sentiment that the government is concealing what it knows about the attacks. The prevalence of this belief seems to be lower in the Nordic countries. In a Swedish survey from 2015, only around 5% of respondents completely or somewhat believed that the US government was behind the 9/11 terrorist attacks (Föreningen Vetenskap och Folkbildning 2015). In Denmark, in a survey from 2017, around 10% of respondents agreed somewhat or completely with a statement that explicitly elaborated what the motives of a conspiratorial US government could have been: 'The American government – with former President George W. Bush at the helm – was behind the terrorist attacks on the World Trade Center on September the 11 in order to have an excuse to start a war in the Middle East and that way secure their access to oil' (Petersen and Osmundsen 2018). Surprisingly, in a survey from 2017 in Iceland, about 16% found it quite or very likely that the attacks had been planned by the US government

10 *Conspiracy theories and Nordic countries*

as opposed to terrorists from the Middle East. There were substantial education and gender differences in those beliefs among Icelanders, with around 21% of males and 13% of females subscribing to this conspiracy theory, and around 24% of those with compulsory education but 9% among those with college degrees (Thorisdottir, forthcoming).

The conspiracy theory that the 1969 moon landing was staged and actually never took place is embraced somewhat or completely by around 6% of Swedes and 12% of Danes (Föreningen Vetenskap och Folkbildning 2015; Petersen and Osmundsen 2018).

Arguably, the conspiracy theory that has circulated in the West with the most potential to cause general harm concerns vaccines. These conspiracy theories revolve around pharmaceutical companies actively suppressing or denying evidence that vaccines, the MMR vaccine in particular, can cause autism or other harmful conditions in children. This theory took hold after 1998 when *The Lancet*, a prestigious medical journal, published a paper by Andrew Wakefield supposedly demonstrating these types of harms. The article was later retracted for, among other things, data manipulation. Since then, although vaccination rates continue to be high, some communities within the Nordic countries have seen a drop in vaccination rates. Although unclear to what degree that can be blamed on conspiracy theories, Iceland and Denmark do not reach the 95% vaccination rate stipulated by the WHO as the minimum to reach herd immunity, although both countries are close at 94%. In fact, in 2018, only 44% of school-age children in Denmark went to school where more than 90% of the students had received the full MMR vaccination dose (Sundhedsstyrelsen 2019). Coinciding with this, new outbreaks of measles have occurred in the Nordics in recent years: 28 people were diagnosed with the disease in Gothenburg, Sweden, in 2018; five in Iceland; and seven in Denmark, both in early 2019 (Sundell, Dotevall, Sansone et al. 2019; Directorate of Health, Iceland 2019). In Denmark, in 2017, a startling 16% of respondents were somewhat or completely in agreement with the statement that the MMR vaccine could cause autism (Petersen and Osmundsen 2018). In Sweden, 7% believe the risk involved in the MMR vaccination is greater than the benefits (Föreningen Vetenskap och Folkbildning 2015).

A rare exception where comparable data exists from all the Nordic countries comes from the 2018 Wellcome Global Monitor (Wellcome Trust 2019), the largest international survey on how people feel about health and science. In the survey, a few questions touched on vaccines, although not specifically in the context of an explicit conspiracy theory. Most notably, one question asked if people agreed or disagreed that vaccines are safe, and another question asked respondents with children,

Conspiracy theories and Nordic countries   11

Table 1.2 Belief in the safety of vaccines

	Vaccines are safe (% who agree)	Your children vaccinated?	Official MMR vaccination rate
Denmark	70%	95%	94%[a]
Finland	73%	98%	96%[b]
Iceland	61%	96%	94%[c]
Norway	83%	97%	96%[d]
Sweden	70%	97%	97%[e]

a www.sst.dk/da/nyheder/2019/~/media/02CBB557937E4218AE5F742CA642FA9B.ashx
b www.thl.fi/roko/rokotusrekisteri/atlas/atlas-en.html?show=infantbc
c www.landlaeknir.is/servlet/file/store93/item37616/Þátttaka%20%C3%AD%20 almennum%20bólusetningum%20barna%20á%20Íslandi%202018.pdf
d www.fhi.no/globalassets/dokumenterfiler/helseregistre/sysvak-dekningsstatistikk-2017–2018/fylker_2-ar_2018.pdf
e www.folkhalsomyndigheten.se/globalassets/smittskydd-sjukdomar/vaccinationer/vaccinationsstatistik-fran-barnhalsovarden-2018_rapport-181022.pdf

if their children had received a vaccine. As can be seen in Table 1.2, beliefs in the safety of vaccines vary noticeably between countries, ranging from a disconcerting low of 61% in Iceland to a high of 83% in Norway, and the reported vaccination rate of own children from 95% to 98%. As a comparison, the lowest of all countries in the survey was France, with only 47% saying vaccines are safe and 91% having vaccinated their children. In Germany, the numbers were similar to the Nordic countries, and in the United States, 72% said vaccines were safe and 93% had vaccinated their children. In this survey, the observed discrepancy between fairly prevalent scepticism about the safety of vaccines yet the high self-reported vaccination rate of own children is interesting. It could stem from people thinking that although vaccines are not completely safe, their benefits outweigh the potential cost. In Norway, around 96% of all two-year-old children were up to date with their vaccines. In 2018, in Denmark, 94% of children had received their first MMR vaccination, but the coverage was down to 89% for the second injection at age four. In Iceland, 94% of children have received the MMR vaccine at 18 months and 95% at 12 years, when the booster vaccine is given in Iceland.

Taken together, the limited data that exists on the prevalence of conspiracy theories in the Nordics seems to indicate that, somewhat surprisingly, they appear to have the highest endorsement in the smallest country, Iceland. Interestingly, Iceland is also the only Nordic country that has suffered a major blow to political trust in the recent decade – possibly hinting at a causal mechanism.

12 *Conspiracy theories and Nordic countries*

Structure of the book

This book is thematically organized. Each chapter looks at different areas of society and social life in which conspiracy beliefs tend to occur. Some of the conspiracy theories involved have had major ramifications (e.g. anti-Semitism); others have had more local effects. They all express underlying conflicts, and we try to tease out their meaning by means of both comparison and contextual readings. The book is a 'first take' on the subject, and, as such, does not attempt to present a comprehensive view of the region. We offer, rather, some snapshots of how and why conspiracy theories have come about and what role they have played, illustrating some of the dynamics involved.

Chapter 2 looks at the role of the state and elite secret societies in Nordic conspiracy beliefs. Secret elites' are central to conspiracy narratives. They have been perceived as pulling the strings behind critical incidents such as the murder of Swedish Prime Minister Olof Palme in 1986, the sinking of the ferry *Estonia* in 1994, and the Norwegian terrorist attacks of 2011. Some of the motifs of these narratives have historical continuity, harking back to the assassination of Swedish King Gustav III in 1792 – which was described as the work of the Knights Templars – or more recent examples such as the occupation of Denmark and Norway during the Second World War. In recent years, 'deep state' conspiracy theories – suggesting that secret networks within the state administration are manipulating political development beyond electoral control, pushing for a society under totalitarian control – have been imported especially from the United States. These narratives can be seen as reactions to globalization and a general sense of loss of control.

Chapter 3 investigates issues of family, gender, and sexuality in the Nordic countries. This chapter traces the history of family reforms from the late nineteenth century which led to specific Nordic forms of welfare regimes and official views and policies on gender and sexuality. Building the 'good' and 'right' kind of family is central to modern nation-state building, since the nation is promoted as the family writ large. The chapter gives examples of how the stresses of these social and political developments have been expressed in conspiracy lore about family, gender, and sexuality over two centuries.

Chapter 4 focuses on migration and the perception of dangerous outsiders and traces anti-immigrant conspiracy theories in the Nordic countries since the oil crisis of 1972, from when the first right-wing populist parties found initial electoral success in the region. Rhetoric on migration and multiculturalism gradually changed from emphasizing openness, equal treatment, and the protecting of human rights

Conspiracy theories and Nordic countries 13

towards requirements of adhering to fundamental values of the native society. One of the most important conspiracy theories discussed in this chapter is the so-called Eurabia theory, the fear of Muslims infiltrating the West in collaboration with domestic traitors. A central believer in the theory was Anders Behring Breivik, who in 2011 massacred 77 of those he thought agents in the plot of subverting Norway and ruining its Christian heritage.

Chapter 5 travels outside the Nordic region and analyzes the conspiratorial images *about* the Nordic countries found in neighbouring countries. Largely leaning on the Nordic region's own repertoire of conspiracy theories, these stories at the same time contribute to creating a particular reputation for the different Nordic countries: the state orchestrating the deterioration of family and sexual norms in Norway, masterminding a migration crisis in Sweden, and promoting bestiality in Denmark; the conspiracy theories about Finland and Iceland have an auxiliary role supporting these tropes. The chapter investigates the most resonating conspiracy narratives about the Nordics, the reasons for their emergence, the means for their distribution, and their impact worldwide.

Chapter 6 offers synthesis and reflection on the issues raised in the preceding five chapters. Is there a Nordic exceptionalism to the conspiracy theories propagated in and about this region? We conclude that although the Nordics have a specific style, which is sometimes less flamboyant than found elsewhere, there is no exceptionalism, no Nordic *Sonderweg*. Conspiracy theories have been part of Nordic history for a very long time with varying intensity, and a variety of plots and perpetrators, as a symptom of an underlying anxiety or anger.

Note

1 Scandinavia comprises, in its usual Nordic usage, Denmark, Norway, and Sweden. Historically, it may include Iceland, Åland, and the Faroe islands, as they include the part of the Nordics that share the Norse language and 'culture' as background. Scandinavism or pan-Scandinavianism is an ideology of inter-/pan-Scandinavian cooperation and/or integration. 'Cultural Nordism' would then include these areas, Greenland (as part of Denmark) *and* Finland, i.e. the region that is elsewhere often called Scandinavia.

2 The state and secret elites in the Nordic countries

State formation processes in the Nordic countries have for more than five centuries developed along fairly stable trajectories. Early conflicts between the kingdoms of Denmark and Sweden were resolved through the establishment of the Nordic Union (1397–1523) and subsequently the existence of independent territorial composite states well into the nineteenth century: Denmark–Norway (until 1814) and Sweden–Finland (1809). As a result of further geopolitical developments, the five Nordic countries – Finland, Sweden, Norway, Iceland, and Denmark – were formed as independent entities during the twentieth century but have retained strong elements of peaceful collaboration and policy alignment. Effective and centralized state bureaucracies and forward-looking reforms set the Nordic countries early onto a path towards modernization, a hallmark of Nordic self-design and perception across the globe.

This is a story of incremental and overall peaceful change based on a spirit of compromise and common sense. It is complicated by also being accompanied by a string of conspiracist imaginaries in which the state as actor has been accused of being controlled by secret elites and exposed to the machinations of secret societies (Åsard 2006: 64). In this chapter, we trace the genealogy of these imaginaries back to the eighteenth century, when fraternal orders like Freemasonry became an integrated part of elite sociability in the two Nordic kingdoms of Denmark and Sweden. Since then, accusations of conspiracy and the existence of a 'deep' or hidden state have been mobilized at occasions of, for example, national crises, such as the murder of Swedish Prime Minister Olof Palme in 1986, the sinking of the ferry MS *Estonia* in 1994, or the Norwegian terrorist attacks of 2011. These events and the conspiracy theories surrounding them can be interpreted as *endogenous responses* to internal crises. However, other substantial features of conspiracy culture in the Nordic countries have originated in external impulses or *exogenous impacts*

16 *The state and secret elites*

and cultural globalization. In this vein, the region has absorbed huge proportions of conspiracy culture circulating on a global scale. In the past decades, these impulses most often originated in the Anglo-Saxon world, with narratives about 9/11 and the war on terror playing a central role, and paving the way for conspiracy theories about 'chemtrails', vaccines, the 5G-net, COVID-19 and much more. All relate to government and state complicity in events and developments that have an adverse effect on an unsuspecting population.

Secret societies

A long-standing trope of conspiracy in the Nordic countries relates to speculation formed around secret societies, most notably Freemasonry. Over the last three centuries conspiratorial fear of secret societies has been mobilized in religious groups across denominations and among political opposition and radicalized fringe groups. Harking back to the eighteenth century and extending into the cyber age, secret societies have been accused of pulling the strings behind political developments, covering up plots, coordinating decision-making in opaque zones of informal economies, or engaging in evil ideology or perverted rituals (Önnerfors 2017b: 105–124). When did this start?

When Swedish Freemasonry took the stage on the occasion of the birth of Swedish Crown Prince Gustav (later King Gustav III), on 13 January 1746, it almost immediately experienced a backlash in the form of the first printed conspiracy theories. Swedish Freemasons struck a medal replete with masonic symbolism and presented it to the royal court. The presentation was reported in the German journal *Europäischer Staats-Secretarius* in 1746, with a translation of the speech delivered on the occasion. Anders von Höpken (1712–1789), Freemason, prominent politician, and an employee of the Office of Foreign Affairs, herein described the expectations directed towards the young prince. It was his task to push back the clouds of ignorance and disunion and to restore a sparkling light of glory for himself and the Swedish name. Von Höpken concluded: 'With one word, and using the language that is peculiar to the secrets of the Freemasons, you will bring the great building of our felicity and its glory to perfection' (Önnerfors forthcoming). But not everyone was equally enthusiastic that a secret society with members within the top echelons of Swedish society was hailing the newborn crown prince. 'Skevikarna', a Protestant sect which by today's standards would be called evangelical–fundamentalist, published a pamphlet in Danzig, *Emot Freymäurerna* – 'Against the Freemasons' (Ericksson 1746) in which they outlined their criticism against the state of affairs in general

The state and secret elites 17

and of Freemasonry in particular. Without going through the 16-page tract in detail – it is saturated with biblical verses and references to God's impending wrath – it suffices to raise a few generic points that place it within the wider genre of conspiracy literature related to Freemasonry and other fraternal orders. These points have recurred in the discourse ever since *Emot Freymäurerna* expressed a general critique against elites engaging in a secret fraternity. The Freemasons, according to the critique, by styling themselves as descendants of Cain and of Solomon, clearly reveal that their intentions are of decadence and destruction. In strong religious language, the tract vehemently expressed the position that divine order is placed over human and that all attempts at human self-mastery are doomed to fail. The Skevik tract attempted to reveal Masonic arcana, what is 'really' behind the ideology of Freemasonry – an agenda of Satanism, heresy, and paganism. The 'Cainite' fraternity, it is asserted, is engaged in an alleged attempt to achieve political world dominance and domination of all religious creeds.

Together with other texts penned by the Skevik sect, their anti-Masonic tract was prohibited by a Swedish royal edict in 1747. It was never very influential. However, the episode represents an early example of a way of thinking where significant events could be interpreted as the outcome of a secret and malevolent elite's association and manipulations. Most of the tropes expressed in *Emot Freymäurerna* have survived well into the twenty-first century.

Despite such critique, Freemasonry and other fraternal forms of sociability flourished in both Nordic kingdoms and their possessions on German territory. They had early and long-lasting involvement as functional elites in politics, administration, and economy. Accusations of conflicting loyalties were expressed in a royal edict in Denmark in 1780 when Swedish prince Duke Karl (later King Karl XIII) assumed leadership of an all-European Knights Templar branch of Freemasonry. Danish members would have been forced to take an oath of fidelity to a foreign prince and this, argued the edict, could potentially lead to inappropriate authority and influence. This royal edict (which explicitly referred to what we today would call negative media accounts) must be interpreted against the backdrop of an all-European debate on secret societies, who were accused of counter-Enlightenment positions, adherence to obscure 'unknown superiors', dubious ritual practices, and malign machinations.

This debate was not least fuelled by the prohibition and persecution of the Bavarian Illuminati in 1785. The central tropes of secret loyalties and malign machinations were finally transformed into full-blown conspiracy theories in the aftermath of the French Revolution,

18   *The state and secret elites*

when enlightened elites were scapegoated for overthrowing the old order of Crown and Church. In Sweden (and the rest of Europe), anti-revolutionary conspiracy theories were mobilized when King Gustav III was assassinated by a group of aristocrats opposed to his increasingly autocratic tendencies (Åsard 2006: 65–70; Önnerfors 2020). Following Prussia (1798) and Great Britain (1799), Sweden in 1803 adopted legislation to control the activities of secret societies. During the first half of the nineteenth century, the old elites in Sweden were accused of utilizing Freemasonry and fraternal orders as a form of political and opaque coterie. At the same time, horrible tales of blood libel were disseminated in folklore and in the press, according to which Freemasons were slaughtering Christian children and sending their blood and corpses to the 'Hundturken' (Dog Turks) to pay off a century-old debt to the Ottoman empire (Bergstrand 1956; Ullgren 2010: 229–242). The prevalence and dissemination of this Islamophobic tale (a variation of the Jewish blood libel but now ascribed to Freemasonry, also explored in the chapters to come) is one of the first instances of a conspiracy theory expressing the belief that Scandinavian elites were involved in a secret plot with the Muslim Other.

Under the influence of the spurious *Protocols of the Elders of Zion*, the early twentieth century witnessed an active reception of the myth of a 'Jewish-Masonic' world conspiracy. A product of multiple influences, the *Protocols* were put together in tsarist Russia, from whence it spread with emigrés in the aftermath of the revolution of 1917. It was adopted by multiple parties in Western Europe. It bolstered different versions of grand conspiracy narratives, not least that of the 'Jewish-Masonic' cabal. The dissemination of this narrative was facilitated in the Nordic countries by the Swedish exile of German general Erich Ludendorff. It was here that he penned his 'stab-in-the-back myth' – that Germany had been defeated by an unholy alliance of domestic enemies – and later on *Die Vernichtung der Freimaurerei durch Enthüllung ihrer Geheimnisse* (The Destruction of Freemasonry through the Revelation of its Secrets) in 1927. It was almost immediately (1928) translated into Swedish and Norwegian, and contributed to popularizing this blend of anti-Semitism and anti-Masonry in Sweden, Norway, and Finland before and during the Second World War. In the latter country, Freemasonry was identified as an anti-nationalist force. In the early 1930s, the brotherhood was accused of involvement in a spectacular murder where the victim was dismembered and the Finnish Church declared the incompatibility of freemasonry with Christianity. In the light of pro-Nazi sentiments and the alliance with Nazi Germany during the war, Finnish Freemasonry came to a complete standstill until 1945 (Ahtokari 2000, 358–360). Although

The state and secret elites 19

Danish and Norwegian Freemasonry was prohibited violently under Nazi occupation, anti-Masonic rhetoric continued to flourish post-1945. The Finnish church was not alone in its critique. There are many instances of evangelical anti-Masonry in the Nordic countries and some spectacular cases of revelations. In Norway in 1994, the theologian Sverre Dag Mogstad published a book on Freemasonry, revealing its rituals. Throughout Scandinavia this exposure sparked considerable attention in the press that tended towards conspiracy speculations. The Swedish tabloid *Expressen* (1995) published a front page with the headline: 'Well-known Swedes Drink Blood in Secret Movement' and listed Freemasons in public life. Since then, the tabloid press in the Nordic countries has regularly published articles on secret societies, and TV documentaries have been produced and screened across Scandinavia.

Mogstad criticized Freemasonry for its secrecy and its possible theological heterodoxy, while other critics were more engaged in local and personal conflicts. These critiques led to higher public interest, and lent some attention to the anti-Masonic conspiracy narratives prominent on the fringes. Jüri Lina, an émigré to Sweden from Estonia, has been prolific in publishing titles in which the politics of Northern Europe are described as the outcome of secret machinations (Lina 2004). According to Lina, Freemasonry has created a vast network of Satanic influence across political systems with the aim of overthrowing national states and natural order. In 2020, Lina rose to new prominence in siding with anti-COVID-19 conspiracy theorists. Radio Islam, a now-defunct Islamist news channel, was established in 1987 and spewed anti-Semitic and anti-Masonic messages for decades. It also published a register of individuals claiming to be involved in the plot. In the digital age, this work has been embraced by Internet platforms such as civilkurage.org or frimurare.info, both of which tap into the political and religious condemnation of Freemasonry or claim that Sweden is a province of the Order of Illuminati.

Was Breivik a tool of a 'Jewish-Masonic' conspiracy?

Claims of conspiracy abound after significant events. So, too, in the aftermath of the terrorist attacks of 22 July 2011. The terrorist Anders Behring Breivik proved to be member of a Norwegian lodge of Freemasons and, in his manifesto, he styled himself a member of the imaginary order 'European Knights Templar'. These connections provided the founding father of Peace and Conflict research, Johan Galtung, fuel to revive old anti-Semitic tropes of the *Protocols of the Elders of Zion* (Galtung 2011; cf. Færseth 2013: 248–251). He and his

20   *The state and secret elites*

Swedish colleague Ola Tunander launched theories that Breivik may have been controlled by the Israeli secret service Mossad in order to torpedo the Oslo Peace Process between Israel and Palestine. For Galtung, it was a plausible explanation that the state of Israel was able to pull the strings of a Freemason in order to carry out a terrorist attack, leaving 77 dead and many more injured and traumatized, most among them being teenagers. Galtung also claimed that the Norwegian Police Security Service (PST) was a 'tool for the abolishment of democracy in Norway'. This was evidenced by, for instance, the PST overlooking Breivik's 'Templar/Masonic-connection', and potentially consciously delaying counterterrorism operations on the day of the attacks (Galtung 2011).

In one of his propositions, Galtung recommended that his audience read books written by the prolific Norwegian conspiracists Per-Aslak Ertresvåg and Erik Rudstrøm (Galtung 2011). Galtung repeatedly cited ideas from Rudstrøm's two-volume work on Freemasonry and secret power elites (Rudstrøm 2005), as well as Ertresvåg's books on similar issues (Ertresvåg 2006; 2008) claiming to identify the existence of a 'deep state' that manipulates domestic and international politics beyond democratic control. It was further claimed that the Norwegian social democratic movement received instructions from 'Jewish Zionism' (as outlined in the *Protocols*), which, as is frequently claimed in conspiratorial literature, uses Freemasonry as its tool.

Tunander, for his part, devoted an entire article to arguing that Breivik essentially acted on behalf of Israeli interests (Tunander 2011). The varied speculations in Tunander's article painted a picture of Breivik as ensnared in an intricate transnational conspiracy between different secret services and criminal networks. According to Tunander, the complexity of Breivik's operation proved that he did not act alone. In their search for all-encompassing explanations, it was obvious that neither Galtung nor Tunander paid particularly close attention to the intellectual home of the perpetrator. Instead, they turned this confessed right-wing mass murderer into a passive victim of external manipulation directed against the Israel-critical foreign politics of Norway.

Both of these academics were met with public criticism. Tunander was sharply rebuked for his speculative endeavours by his then-employer, the Peace Research Institute of Oslo. Galtung was already retired and was criticized, but the public attention to his legitimation of anti-Semitic sources (e.g. Færseth 2013: 250–251) led to a further decline in his reputation. However, such activity did contribute to mainstreaming claims that had belonged to the fringes. This was partially due to the fact that the fringe culture had recently become more relevant to the mainstream through interpretations of external events like 9/11 and the war

The state and secret elites   21

on terror. But interest in hidden hands and secret plots had also been activated by internal events.

Theories of trauma – Palme and the MS *Estonia*

Big, traumatic events often make people search for equally big, meaningful causes. This proportionality bias can lead to the construction of conspiracy narratives, especially when real causes do not satisfy the bias, or they continue to be somewhat obscure. Few events in recent Nordic history illustrate this like the aftermath of the murder of then-Swedish Prime Minister Olof Palme.

Following a night out at the movies, Olof Palme was shot and killed in central Stockholm on 28 February 1986. Despite massive efforts made in the subsequent murder investigation (officially closed in 2020), the perpetrator was never apprehended and the motive thus never established with certainty. Instead, the killing of Olof Palme unleashed a plethora of conspiracy theories, many of them accusing secret elites or a 'deep state' of a deliberate assassination plot and suppression of the truth – somewhat like, and somewhat inspired by, the conspiracy theories about the murder of JFK (see Åsard 2006).

The details of the Palme murder triggered much speculation: Why was there no bodyguard? Was it only one perpetrator? Why did it take time before the Swedish mass media informed the public? Why was the police investigation slow to start, and why was it so badly carried out? Åsard (2006) points out that the murder of Palme came as a complete shock and paralyzed the nation, including its functional elites. The police investigation was driven deductively. Rather than focusing on available evidence at the crime scene, it started from potential motives that ranged from completely random assumptions to advanced international political plots. This fuzziness encouraged conspiracy thinking. An early theory, followed by the investigation, was that Palme was the victim of a politically motivated assassination carried out by Kurdish terrorists. When that theory collapsed, suspicion was directed towards a 'lone wolf', Christer Pettersson. A chronic substance abuser and known, violent petty criminal, he was initially convicted for the murder in a district court in 1989, but exonerated in the Crown Court.

Over the years, four governmental commissions have assessed the multiple failures of police and judicial authorities regarding the case. One of the reasons for these voluminous investigation was to counter public distrust – partially in the form of conspiracy theories – and to ensure democratic transparency. One of the largest, the so-called *Granskningskommissionen*, between 1994 and 1999, produced a

22   *The state and secret elites*

thousand-page report addressing shortcomings and potential missed opportunities in the search for perpetrators, including some details common in conspiracy narratives. Among these are, for instance, indications that reactionary circles inside the Swedish security agencies might be responsible for the assassination. Although celebrated as an international statesman epitomizing social democratic values, in Sweden considerable hatred was directed against Palme, his politics, and his personality. This hatred had its own name, *Palmehat*, and it was a feature of the discourse in extremely conservative and nationalist circles. As late as 2009, an allegedly 'satirical' drinking song hailing the murder of Palme and deriding the subsequent police investigation was still very popular among conservative and radical right party members (Åkesson 2009a).

In conspiracist readings of the murder, *Palmehat* was identified as the ideological glue of an alleged deep-state plot, orchestrated by police and security services (Åsard 2006: 193–215). The main champion of this thesis was journalist Sven Anér, who over the years produced voluminous accounts of an internal conspiracy involving the highest echelons of the Swedish state apparatus. He was far from alone: since 2010, the website palmemordet.se has been gathering information related to the different theories. Their related podcast, *Palmemordet*, as of 2021 counted no fewer than 254 episodes (Palmemordet 2020), and from time to time, mainstream national and international media return to the many questions that remain unsolved more than three decades after the event (Mortimore 2011; West-Knights 2019).

On social media, the murder still occupies the minds of people searching for conclusive answers ranging from falsifiable evidence to conspiracist guesswork. They even have their own social network, *privatspanarna* – the 'private investigators' – a sect-like organization (mostly men) committed to solving the crime and 'fuelling a cottage industry of Palme mania' or 'Palmology' (West-Knights 2019). As West-Knights points out, the investigation has turned into one of the largest in the world, including on a psychological level: 'the mystery of Palme's death has become a national obsession', also called *Palmesjukdom* – Palme sickness' – leading some 130 people to confess to the crime. It is in the margins between the magnitude of the crime, the obvious incompetency with which the investigation was carried out at the governmental level, and the amount of trauma in self-perception Sweden experienced that a hotbed for more or less unlimited speculation was created and where it still proves fertile. As a Swedish government official put it as early as 1997: 'Our problem is what the people of Sweden believe happened and how they deal with that' (West-Knights

The state and secret elites 23

2019). The narrative of government failure, allegations of malevolent plots, and diabolic deception may have primed the public, because only a few years later, another event also unleashed conspiracy theories on a large scale.

Between 27 and 28 September 1994 the ferry MS *Estonia*, carrying 989 passengers between Tallinn, Estonia, and Stockholm, Sweden, sank in the Baltic Sea. It had been hit by harsh weather and Force 9 gales, causing enormous waves (Åsard 2006: 70–85), but the precise mechanisms of the disaster have never been established with certainty. This, and other aspects of the aftermath, has invited conspiracist explanations.

Most passengers lost their lives. A Mayday call was released shortly after midnight, but when the rescue mission commenced, it was only possible to save 137 lives. Investigations were seen as hampered. In the period between two governments in Sweden, both the outgoing and the incoming prime minister decided in December 1994 to recover neither the MS *Estonia* nor the bodies of the victims and instead to declare the area in the Baltic Sea a sanctuary, basically a maritime graveyard. Many survivors and relatives of the deceased protested against the decision. The report of the joint Finnish–Estonian–Swedish international disaster committee was finally released in 1997. It placed blame on the German dockyard Meyer Werft for construction problems, and the dock loaders in Tallinn for loading so the ferry encountered high waves from the wrong angle, damaging the weakest point in the construction of the hull.

Such prosaic explanations did not satisfy the proportionality bias, and so a string of 'reports' have been released that more or less all diverge from the official international commission. Some of them are clearly conspiratorial in nature, ranging from plausible to entirely wild claims. The most prominent alternative theory is that the MS *Estonia* was sabotaged. Journalist and writer Knut Carlqvist (2001) advanced the explanation that the ferry was exposed to a bomb attack or hit by an explosive device. He claimed that vehicles loaded with military equipment were on board, leading him to assume that Russian weaponry was intended to be transported via Estonia to Sweden and beyond. Carlqvist assembled statements of survivors, but only those who supported his theories, and he never elaborated his own evidence but pointed to the inaccessibility of information as proof of a malignant cover-up.

Another explanation was provided by shipbuilding engineer Anders Björkman (1998), who claimed that the bow visor was removed deliberately and that the ferry was actually hit under the waterline. Björkman

24 *The state and secret elites*

argued that the disaster was covered up by a political conspiracy and that the public has been lied to, subjected to disinformation and manipulated deliberately, orchestrated by the Swedish Civil Contingency Agency (MSB) colluding with civil and military secret services. One of his comrades-in-arms is the Swedish-German lawyer and author Henning Witte. He added to Björkman's claims that the ferry might have been hit by a Russian torpedo fired from a submarine in order to thwart the export of sensitive military technology.

In his analysis of the MS *Estonia* conspiracy narratives, Åsard (2006) identified four recurring traits. First, the government's unwillingness to document the damage of the wreck and recover its load was seen as suspicious. Secondly, conspiracy writers showed an over-occupation with technical details. Thirdly, the description of a devious Other (government, state actors, unspecified supreme 'interests', or even named individuals) was deemed as dangerous and an almost omnipotent and diabolic enemy. Fourthly, conspiracy writers underlined that there was a massive plot between political stakeholders and the media to cover up their evil action.

The episode concerning the MS *Estonia* could have remained of interest to an esoteric circle of truth-seekers only, such as *privatspanarna* in the case of Palme. But for the Swedish radical right, the MS *Estonia* proved a platform for political propaganda that couldn't be ignored. In 2016, yet another book, *M/S* Estonia*: The Disaster of the Swedish State*, was released by sea captain and nationalist politician Stefan Torsell through the publishing house AlternaMedia. It distributes titles denying climate change, decrying political correctness, and promoting conspiracy theories of social, political and economic collapse, and of the so-called Identitarian movement and 'post-democracy'. Among the authors, we find Swedish, Russian, Estonian, and Danish conspiracy theorists and right-wing activists such as Katarina Janouch, 'Julia Caesar (a former journalist writing under pseudonyme)', Alexandr Dugin, Lars Hedegaard, and the above-mentioned Jüri Liina.

Torsell's book on the MS *Estonia* was heavily promoted by AlternaMedia, most likely because it captured a widespread conspiracy narrative of a corrupt Swedish government plotting against its own population. This idea had gained traction in the aftermath of the 2015 refugee crisis (see Chapter 4). Beyond the more fanciful titles released by the publishing house, the recycling of already established conspiracy theories related to the MS *Estonia* promised to appeal to a more technically inclined, mostly male, audience. This audience identified the 1994 disaster as a cover-up that could be proven by 'hard facts' and belonged more to the technocratic than the ideologically motivated faction of the

The state and secret elites   25

Swedish radical right. Talk about an imminent systemic collapse was omnipresent, and the Swedish radical right capitalized on Estonia as an already established conspiracy narrative to serve as yet more proof of diabolic deception.

Another kind of trauma: 9/11 Truth and the war on terror

Big, internal events in the Nordic countries have thus certainly contributed to making conspiracy theories available as an everyday topic. But these event narratives and their larger frames have often been influenced by and sometimes directly imported from abroad. No single recent event contributed as much to establishing Americanized conspiracy culture in the Nordics as did the events on 11 September 2001 and the ensuing war on terror. As the events coincided with a more interactive Internet where user-made content became widely distributed, fear, rumours, explanations, and celebrity travelled faster and become more easily visible. Conspiracy culture anchored itself in a diversity of sites, on- and offline, strengthened by geopolitical developments.

The change in global geopolitics following the wars in Afghanistan and Iraq served as a catalyst for adopting and disseminating conspiracy theories about state malfeasance and corruption because the plot and consequence of these theories were no longer restricted to the United States. In different scale and scope, Nordic countries participated in the different theatres of war, most notably in Iraq and in Afghanistan, and saw the direct consequences of warfare when caskets of fallen soldiers were returned home. Domestically, fear of Islamic terrorism led to increased suspicion towards immigrants and refugees (see Chapter 4), as well as increased surveillance and debates about civil rights versus national security. All these topics have been present in how the conspiracy theories of 9/11 have been defended and disseminated over the years, with the financial crisis of 2008 adding to the mix. Debate over the events of 9/11 has, in other words, been drawn into ever-larger narratives on the way the world secretly works, with villains including everyone from the more narrowly defined US administrations to the Masons and the Jews. Conspiracy culture being what it is, this led to conflict, with some focusing narrowly on events and causes, some broadening out to larger political issues, and some entertaining a 'big picture' that included UFOs and a spiritual breakthrough (cf. Dyrendal 2017).

They could participate in the so-called Truther movement started in the United States, most notably 9/11 Truth (911truth.org), Architects and Engineers for 9/11 Truth (ae911truth.org), and Scholars for 9/11 Truth and Justice (stj911.org). Similar local groups were set up

26   *The state and secret elites*

in Western European countries, and the Nordic countries were no exception. Norway had two: one comprised of 'conspiritual' activists (Dyrendal 2017) and the other of secular-minded people who had little patience for spiritual messages from UFOs and the super-conspiracy theories of the former. To some extent, however, they shared the general political critique of the global political and economic order. While the scene was not without right-wing activists, the central actors were mostly left-leaning with some libertarians mixed in. In Denmark as well, the left dominated the scene, while the most visible actors in Sweden were part of an alternative conspiracist scene with a generous contribution from the far right.

Most of the conspiracy beliefs were adopted directly from the US discourse, and Nordic conspiracy discourse ran the gamut of the US scene. The former leader of the Norwegian *Socialist Left*, retired professor of social psychology Berit Ås, fronted the 'no planes' theories – that no planes were involved in the destruction of the Twin Towers. She also advocated, like most conspiracists, that the towers instead fell due to a controlled demolition. Although the controlled demolition element was more popular than 'no planes', the combination was not uncommon. In Nordic conspiracy discourse, the theory that the US government 'let it happen on purpose' was not as common as they 'made it happen on purpose' (cf. Olmsted 2010: 221–222). Just *who* these actors that made or let it happen on purpose were, varied. While most were happy to blame either the Bush administration or a shadowy deep state, parts of the far right and parts of the far left were eager to include Israel or simply 'the Jews'.

Internationally and in the Nordic countries, conspiracy theories eventually centred on the collapse of a building not hit directly by any plane. World Trade Center 7 (WTC7) was the third building in the complex to fall almost seven hours after it was hit by debris from the North Tower. Its almost symmetrical, extremely rapid collapse, and the absence of any airplane collision, confirmed suspicions of foul play for conspiracy theorists. Only a series of controlled demolitions could have brought it down claimed Utah physicist Steven E. Jones (Jones 2006) and former theology professor David Ray Griffin (Griffin 2004). A video of Steven Jones lecturing about WTC7 reached Danish chemist Niels Harrit around 2007. Formerly an associate professor at the University of Copenhagen, Harrit became the main spokesperson of the Danish Truther movement, as well as a recognized academic authority on the controlled-demolition thesis in the international Truther community. Like many others, his major motivation to engage with this topic was political. Danish troops participated in the American-led wars in

The state and secret elites 27

Afghanistan and in Iraq, and domestically, increased surveillance and civil rights violations were extremely unpopular on the left wing of the political spectrum.

Harrit initially laid out his views in an op-ed about WTC7 in the Danish newspaper *Information*. He presented three major features that would become programmatic for Danish 9/11 conspiracy theories (Harrit 2007). First, the article argued that the official version of how WTC7 collapsed was incorrect. There had to be another explanation, and this should form the basis for a new investigation. It more than suggested that foul play by the US government was at work. Second, it argued that the press – what conspiracy theorists today call the mainstream media – concealed the truth, perhaps in collusion with the government. This made independent research by concerned citizens necessary in order to discover the truth. Third, the op-ed distanced itself from the 'conspiracy theory' label, and initiated a quest to present thoroughly researched findings that could be acceptable to mainstream audiences.

Harrit soon joined Steven Jones in an attempt at proving the controlled-demolition thesis. Jones and others had collected what was said to be timely dust samples from the site in the years following 9/11, and he had already speculated that perhaps so-called superthermite was used to cut the support beams in the towers (Jones 2006: 31). Under the leadership of Jones and Harrit, the dust samples were now subjected to a closer investigation, the results of which were published in a 2009 article co-written with seven other scientists (Harrit et al. 2009).

The article reported findings of red-grey chips in the dust, which was categorized as unexploded thermitic material, or *nano-thermite*. This met immediate critique. These findings were not unproblematic as the chips' signature showed they need not be nano-thermite – they could actually be paint flakes (Thomas 2011). Other items of critique were related to the undocumented chain of custody for the samples, and the venue in which the article was published. The Harrit et al. article was published in 2009 in *The Open Chemical Physics Journal*, widely seen as part of a predatory press. The editor, French professor of nanoscience Marie-Paule Pileni, resigned in protest over the publishing of the article, which she claims happened without her knowledge (Hoffmann 2009). The journal has since been discontinued.

Nevertheless, the 'nano-thermite' explanation became a much-used talking point in international Truther discourse, and Harrit became an international celebrity for believers and infamous to others. The explanation fared badly with experts. The official investigation explicitly tested theories of controlled demolition for WTC7 and dismissed them. Falling

28 *The state and secret elites*

debris and ensuing fire that weakened the steel frame was found to be more than enough to explain the eventual collapse, and the absence of sound levels exceeding 130 dB alone excluded demolition (NIST 2019).

The press and the public

A major mission of Harrit and the 9/11 Truther community, both the Danish and the international ones, has been to engage with the public to convince them of the Truther version of the 9/11 narrative. The rhetorical and media strategies chosen may again be illustrated by Harrit's example.

In terms of media, Harrit attempted to reach the public directly, through a large number of public lectures, but he also reached out through both mainstream and alternative channels. The attempts at using mainstream media may seem surprising. Harrit, like many other conspiracy believers, has been vocal about suspicions that the mainstream media is conspiring with the government in refusing to reveal the real reasons behind 9/11 or to give column inches or airtime to in-depth debate. Reaching out thus gives a rhetorical win-win situation: publication gives access to a new public, while lack of interest from the mainstream media strengthens the narrative of being silenced.

It is inaccurate, however, that the mainstream Danish media has refused to publish or air views by Harrit and other Truthers and the subject of 9/11. Harrit's name appeared at least 80 times in the major Danish daily newspapers from 2007 to 2019, but it is nevertheless clear that the attention given has tended to be one of curiosity with a fringe phenomenon. Consequently, Harrit has moved a lot of his press-related activities to alternative media, such as the *Daily Worker* (Dagbladet Arbejderen) a non-mainstream newspaper published by the Danish Communist Party, and conspiracy-oriented online media in Denmark and abroad. Such alternative venues have been the main channels for spreading conspiracist readings of 9/11 and the aftermath throughout the Nordic countries, often drawing directly on similar sources from abroad. Harrit, for instance, participated in Truther-affiliated YouTube channels, websites, and other outlets, including an appearance on the right-wing *Alex Jones Show* in 2009 to talk about the article on nano-thermite (*Alex Jones Show*, 2009).

The discourse on how the truth is being covered up and 'critics' are being silenced relates to a discourse on victimhood that is central to conspiracy culture, both in the Nordic countries and elsewhere. We can see this in a much-publicized quarrel between Harrit and Danish journalist Søren K. Villemoes, which resulted in a defamation lawsuit

The state and secret elites 29

brought by Harrit. Villemoes had protested an exhibition at the Royal Library in Denmark about the Armenian genocide by the Ottoman Empire (ca. 1914–1923), in which the Turkish Embassy in Denmark had been allowed to add material to the exhibit questioning the validity of the events described as genocide. Villemoes asked rhetorically whether 'Niels Harrit and the other crackpots' from the 9/11 Truther movement should also be invited to present their views at future events, as well as creationists and Holocaust deniers (Villemoes 2012). Harrit lost in the district court in 2013 as well as his appeal in the Eastern High Court in 2015.

The verdict and the way in which it was reported by most media outlets could be seen as both a curse and a blessing for Harrit and the 9/11 Truthers. It was clear that the legitimacy that they were hoping to gain from a victory was not forthcoming, but this simultaneously confirmed Harrit's and the Truthers' narrative about the mainstream media and other elite groups within society. The verdict thus reinforced their status as underdog, locked in a romantic fight for the truth with a far superior, sinister force.

While conspiracy theories, including about 9/11, may relate to more ultimate concerns and use apocalyptic language, most varieties of 9/11 Trutherism appeal first to a rhetoric of rationality, truth, and evidence. Harrit is a clear example of this. He largely went back to spreading his version of the events of 9/11 in his public lectures and in the alternative press, where he was far more successful than in the mainstream outlets.

Harrit's has given his Danish-language public three-hour lectures on WTC7 over 250 times since 2007 and he also tours with a shorter English-language version (Harrit 2017 and Harrit 2013). In his lectures, he is careful initially to state that he only looks at the collapse of WTC7 from a technical and natural scientific angle with reference to Newtonian physics. The overall argument is the same as he originally unfolded in the 2007 op-ed: the towers were brought down via controlled demolition using nano-thermite and other incendiaries and explosives. Harrit is careful and methodical, presents the collected evidence, and tells a compelling story.

The rhetoric of rationality and science is an effective way to manage the potential stigma of conspiracy beliefs (cf. Thalmann 2019), and thus a valued source of legitimizing claims. It may, however, break down. Audience members at Harrit's talks range from acolytes to critics, and by sampling a few video recordings of the lectures, it becomes apparent that although most of the attendees are curious, interested, and sceptical of the official version of events, some also pose hard-hitting questions to Harrit afterwards. In a lecture in Aalborg, the fourth-largest city in

30 *The state and secret elites*

Denmark, Harrit received mixed questions towards the end of the lecture. Some wanted him to express personal opinions about who was behind the attacks. This he refused to do, though he categorically denied that al-Qaeda had anything to do with it. He went further and asserted that while there might have been airplanes, they were not flown by terrorists. No plane hit the Pentagon, he claimed, and the plane that went down in Shanksville, Pennsylvania, was shot down by the military instead of being brought down by the passengers (Harrit 2017). When asked questions critical of his own conclusions, Harrit initially reverted back to a long-held Truther movement talking point, namely the need for a new and impartial investigation of 9/11. In addition, he pointed out that no Danish technical or scientific research group had expressed any interest in discussing his ideas. To him, this was proof that they agreed with him but would face serious consequences from their universities if they stated so publicly. When the critical questions persisted, Harrit still refused to consider other explanations than his own and proceeded to end the session.

Meaning and impact

Conspiracy beliefs are robustly tied to levels of distrust in society. They follow and strengthen distrust in the actors blamed for whatever is going wrong. Following the wars in Afghanistan and (especially) Iraq, trust in American official explanations and the Nordic governments joining them in war fell further among those already critical. Still, the Nordic countries continue to be high-trust societies, and while big events generate the search for big causes, these needs are muted over time. So how much has attention and activity translated into beliefs?

Apparently not all that much. A recent study of Danish attitudes to conspiracy theories found that less than 4% agreed fully with the conspiracy theories that 9/11 was an inside job perpetrated by the American government, with another 6% partially agreeing and 15% undecided (Petersen and Osmundsen 2018). The numbers are similar to Norwegian responses to less sharply phrased questions, while Swedish data show only 1% fully agreeing. The numbers of Swedes who agree partially or have no opinion are also lower at 4% and 8%. The Estonia conspiracy theories fare even worse, with a mere 2% at any level of agreement (VoF 2015: 19). There are few early surveys, but activity and interest around conspiracy theories related to this particular event seem to have died down. The Finnish 9/11 Truther group is all but dead, and the Norwegian activists have almost all moved on, as have the websites and outlets that devoted much attention to these theories. In Denmark,

The state and secret elites 31

a magazine, *KONSPIRATION* (the Danish word for 'conspiracy'), built on the success of the 9/11 Truther movement, saw the light of day in January 2017. It published four issues over the course of 12 months before ceasing publication due to waning sales. It has a continued online presence on social media, however.

This does not mean there has been no cultural impact. The activation of groups of online 'prosumers' of conspiracy culture has led to increased availability of conspiracy narratives as a cultural resource. This is visible, for example, through the increased amount of both worry and jokes about conspiracy theories and their believers. Conspiracy theories also *seem* increasingly prominent as they are presented, shared, and talked about on social media, although the vast amount of attention is critical (cf. Uscinski and Parent 2014). But the mere presence of these theories in books, print, everyday conversations, and social media is an interesting phenomenon. A number of readers and followers will quite plausibly simply be curious and not convinced of the existence of nefarious schemes and plots orchestrated by governments or secret elites. Nevertheless, they reveal a view of the world in which the social contract between the rulers and the ruled is questioned. The mistrust of elites spills over into systemic conspiracy theories about medicine, climate science, economics, and international relations, feeding into populist and authoritarian politics. Notions of truth, authority, sincerity, and basic humanity are constantly questioned. To the venues of conspiracy culture, any event could be a 'false flag', whether the attacks on Charlie Hebdo, Utøya, or the synagogue in Copenhagen. Vaccines were universally 'questioned' for their ties to both big money and government sponsorship. Politicians and scientists engaged in promoting remedies or claims opposing conspiracy beliefs were tied to sinister, secret organizations bent on domination.

As responses to internal crises, societal traumas, and domestic tensions, the conspiracy theories covered here attempt to direct focus on powerful elites. They mostly distort, rather than primarily displace, locus of conflict, focusing blame on both global and local elites, rather than external, weaker scapegoats (cf. Butter 2014). It is mainly within these internal contexts that their meaning is shaped, negotiated, and reproduced for various purposes over time. Outside Sweden, the Palme assassination barely represents proof of the existence of a 'deep state'. On the other hand, we have seen how conspiracy theories in the Nordic countries also are placed within predominantly exogenous contexts of meaning: the Nordic 9/11 Truthers are tapping into international narratives of distrust. These narratives, however, resonate within domestic groups prone to suspicion (of American politics) and individual gatekeepers, translating the global to the local.

3 Family, gender, and sexuality

The site was just outside the capital of Stockholm, Sweden, in the municipality of Södertälje. It had been a long, cold January, with temperatures frequently creeping below -20C. Investigators went to work in the freezing cold and on ground that would not thaw. 'Here, the Police Search for 25 Dead Children', a headline screamed. The story continued: 'The search was to be secret. For two weeks the police have been digging in search of buried children'. This was *Aftonbladet*, the major Swedish tabloid, which reported on 9 February 1993.

The police were searching in good faith. In November 1992, a researcher had gone public with claims that 'devil-worshippers have conducted ritual murder in Sweden' (Aftonbladet, 25.11.1992). This was one case to prove the claims. A young girl, whose father had recently been convicted of incest, said she had been forced to take part in organized child sex abuse in urban brothels, including mass Satanic ritual abuse followed by ritual murder and cannibalism. A large number of refugee children had gone missing, and on questioning, she had agreed that the victims looked foreign. And the Södertälje case was not unique. In a parallel case in the north of Sweden, another girl accused her father and 20 others of rape and sexual abuse, and of being part of a sect committing ritual murders.

The mass media became frantic, with screaming headlines and stories about Satanism, rape, and human sacrifice. The police, however, found no traces of hidden child brothels, no trace of the other men and women supposedly involved, and no traces of buried children. Similar excavations from similar testimony were conducted multiple times later, in other Nordic countries, with identical results (Kringstad 2007)

The 'Södertälje case' had an enormous impact on, and polarized, the public debate in Sweden. At least five books, a number of documentaries, radio programmes, and newspaper articles discussed this case, alone or in combination with other, similar allegations. Critics claimed that a network of extreme feminists was fomenting false accusations. Believers staunchly

34 *Family, gender, and sexuality*

maintained claims about the presence of organized ritual abuse of children, and a conspiracy to hide such horrors. Both conservative evangelicals and radical feminists were propagating claims of a Satanic conspiracy, although they had very different diagnoses of causes and cures.

The debate followed international patterns. Critics stressed rationality, a lack of evidence, and Enlightenment ideals of knowledge production. Evangelicals and radical feminists called for defending and believing the victims (cf. Haaken 1998). The first group questioned the evidential basis for specific allegations and how they were elicited; the other defended them. International debates over memory, testimony, and truth-finding became part of this Nordic debate. This in turn evoked struggles over ideologies of gender, power, and sexuality, blending a moral discourse on belief as solidarity with 'victims' with questions about truth and evidence (see e.g. Guillou 2002; Lundgren 1994).

The allegations of Satanic conspiracy above are among the few conspiracy beliefs relating to family, sexuality, and gender that have been the subject of research in the Nordic context. They echo previous concerns about the debasement of innocents, ritual murder, and cannibalism. Norman Cohn (1975) analyzed such claims from antiquity through the early modern period, in allegations against heterodox Christians, Jews, and 'witches', and called them 'Europe's inner demons'. We find similar stories in the Nordic countries over time. The Swedish cases from the 1990s echo the allegations of sexual transgression in witches' Sabbaths that reached epidemic proportions in Sweden in 1668–1675 (Ankarloo 1987), with fear of and trials for devil worship, murder, child kidnapping, and orgies in secret cabals of witches.

The conspiracy beliefs of the 1990s thus echo aspects of earlier suspicions. Topics related to family, sexuality, and gender are at the heart of every society, since here the intimate and private intersect with issues of great public concern and interest. We therefore find structural and topical similarities, but we also find deeper discontinuities. To paraphrase an old adage: conspiracy narratives are like history in that they rarely repeat (exactly), but they frequently rhyme. The way they rhyme reveals recurring topics of concern and effective tropes of demonization; the way they differ reveals the central, historically situated actors, their context, and the underlying conflicts. Conspiracy beliefs about bodies and their relation are all about contexts of embodied actors, so let us start with some context.

Family reforms to save the family

As discussed in Chapter 1, the Nordic countries are strongly associated with economic prosperity, welfare policies, and individual rights. However, until the middle of the nineteenth century, the region was

Family, gender, and sexuality 35

mainly rural, accommodating an agrarian economy with widespread poverty. Mass emigration followed. Compared to much of Europe, economic modernization was rapid, and developed in parallel with democratization. There was comparatively little elite resistance to these changes. The influence of the Nordic Lutheran churches, intertwined with the state, decreased. Strong popular political, religious, social, and cultural movements developed and became influential. But the freedom and rights of women, and in particular married women, was still under debate (Melby et al. 2006:13). Among the elite there was widespread worry that the family was in crisis. Marriage and birth rates were low; disease and ill health were rife.

In nationalist discourse, the nation is typically promoted as a family writ large. Healthy families are thus an essential component for a successful nation. From the middle of the nineteenth century, worry over the perceived need to build the good and right kind of family in the Nordic countries led to debates about family law reform. Women had traditionally been very important as economically active, and as providers in the largely agrarian Nordic societies. Yet there had been resistance to granting women – especially married women – full civil rights. Gradually, however, through a unique Nordic legal collaboration, starting in 1870 and continuing for about 60 years, women not only became legally equal to men, but obtained civil rights which were more far reaching than in other parts of Europe. In 1880, for example, Danish women obtained control of their own money (Ravn and Rosenbeck 2010: 42).

In the Nordic countries, nationalism and the struggle for women's rights emerged simultaneously (Melby et al. 2006: 51). Public administration increasingly encroached upon the domain of the different national Lutheran churches. In 1908, for instance, it became legal to contract a civil marriage in Sweden. The church also lost its right to play a role in the dissolution of marriage. By the early twentieth century the Nordic countries were unique in granting no-fault divorce. But a stable marriage was still the social and national ideal, and the mutual right of spouses to property increased. The status of children born out of wedlock also improved considerably in this period, and the father became obliged to support such children.

This rapid modernization and urbanization had cultural and social repercussions. Stress and strain were intermittently expressed through conspiracy theories or rumours.

Conspiracy rumours about ritual murder and cannibalism in the nineteenth century

In September 1869, a rumour erupted into mass protests against the central Masonic lodge in Kristiania (Norway's later capital, Oslo).

36   *Family, gender, and sexuality*

Over several evenings, police arrested around 80 protesters. The rioters were angry, anxious, and their concerns were serious. According to the rumours, Freemasons had kidnapped and murdered several young people and sold their bodies to 'Turks' of local folklore – *tryntyrken* in Norwegian; *hundturken* in Swedish – for use in cannibalistic meals. At least four young people were missing and presumed dead by such means (Granrud 2003).

By 1869, the content of such rumours was already old. The version linking Freemasons and Turks to murder and cannibalism respectively had circulated both in Norway and Sweden for more than 50 years. In nineteenth-century Sweden, the rumours came with a nationalist and nativist interpretation: the Turks wanted Swedish, Christian meat in order to rise above themselves. Interestingly, Granrud finds no such tales from Denmark.

On the surface, the conspiracy rumours about Freemasons and Turks seem much like the 1990s allegations about Satanism and ritual murder. Both sets of stories revolve around murder and cannibalism. The perpetrators are secretive groups of (mostly) wealthy and powerful people, while the victims are mostly young, innocent and female. Such common patterns are important. As noted by Jeffrey Victor (1993), motifs of threats to 'children' are expressions of anxiety about the future. Threats directed against the most vulnerable in society are a call to action directed to those culturally encoded as responsible and active; thus, women and children are depicted as ideal victims.

Similarities can also mask contextual differences relating to social change. As long as the anti-Masonic narratives' victims were those of legend, that is, an unnamed 'someone known by a friend of a friend', they were commonly described as having recently moved from the countryside to the city. For example, the chaplain at Akershus castle noted in his 1813 diary that 'silly rumours' held among 'common people' both in urban and rural communities alleged that young and well-fed females could be lured into cities to be slaughtered and sold (Granrud 2003). The rumours thus express anxieties about rapid social change, such as urbanization, and its consequences. The female victims may, at the most essential and general level, reflect a fear of the family losing control over female fertility. Historically, adult family members in rural areas could have cause to be anxious about the fate of young females moving to the city. They would be both outside the immediate control of the family and vulnerable to the financial difficulties of city life. Read less literally through related conspiracy rumours, similar tales of hidden alliances targeting young females are known from, for example, France, where Jews were said to kidnap young girls and send them into prostitution in the Levant (Kapferer

2013). At that level, the 'cannibalism' rumours may reflect the fear of losing the young (women) to other foreign and perverted pleasures.

We should, however, not overlook that trade and commercial transactions are central elements in these conspiracy tales. First, the tales were told and reproduced primarily in rural areas and influenced commercial behaviour in at least some known cases. People embracing the tales refused to trade in the city. This reduced competition in the central city and led to increased prices (Granrud 2003). A common interpretation in media of the time was that the narratives were strategically employed for motives of profit.

The long-lived conspiracy rumour also reveals long-standing societal tension. Poverty was common in Norway and the secretive Freemasons were thought to be rich and powerful. At the same time, egalitarian ideals were rising through this period (Myhre 2018). The Masonic 'riches' were explained as the result of nefarious deeds, an explanation for wealth that is common in societies and among social groups with egalitarian ideals. Such stories of immorality express the ideal of social equality while asserting the reality of vast differences.

Family, gender, and the state 1900–1940

The reforms of the late nineteenth and the early twentieth century probed deeply into the private lives of citizens and aimed to support modernization of society. Early in the period, industrialization increased, and the farmer's movements decreased in political importance compared to labour organizations. Nationalism became more reactionary as the constitution of society changed at a rapid pace. Increasingly science, rather than religion, was used to legitimize developments. The national churches were still important and membership was more or less obligatory, but gradually medical doctors replaced the clergy as the experts of family life, gender roles, sexuality, and the upbringing of children.

Concomitant to extending individual rights to women and children, the *quality* of citizens became a national concern. Social engineering – associated with Social Democracy from the 1930s – had started in the first decade of the twentieth century. The population constituted the raw material from which new modern citizens would emerge, given the right kind of carrot and stick. The dark side of modernization in the form of eugenics played an important role in the reform of family law. Individuals considered substandard were not allowed to marry and were discouraged – or forbidden – to have children. There were, for example, programmes of sterilization in Norway, Denmark, and Sweden.

38 *Family, gender, and sexuality*

As noted above, motifs of threats to children and those considered vulnerable are expressions of anxiety about the future. But anxiety about the future can also be expressed through the fear that youth and young adults will not shoulder responsibility. In the 1920s, critique was directed against young Nordic urban women adopting a foreign flapper, *backfisch*, or *garçonne* style (Myrvang 2003). The androgynous look of the short-haired young women, their 'male' public behaviour (smoking, driving), and their conquering of an earlier male job market was strongly criticized.

Little of this critique was conspiracist. While the far right could encompass this phenomenon in its general world view of a Judeo–Bolshevik–Masonic conspiracy against the *Volk* (see below), mainstream conservatives saw change more as a troubling expression of the zeitgeist. The kings of fashion, expressed one ladies' journal in 1926, were the servants of time, not its masters (in Bjerkan 2009: 31). This did not lessen the controversies. In the troubled times of the late 1930s and the early 1940s there were intense public debates focusing on the problematic youth. In Sweden, middle-class and conservative debaters were horrified by the emerging youth culture. Interest in new styles of music and dancing, and new forms of public display of sexuality, indicated that young people – especially the working class – refused to grow up and accept their position in life; vulgar and imported forms of pleasure posed a direct threat to the survival of a healthy youth and healthy society (see Frykman 1988). This discourse tried to promote simple and nationalistic pastimes, and the authorities were pushed into commissioning studies to scrutinize and plan for the development of a socially and politically healthy youth.

The roles of secular professional experts in the twentieth century multiplied with the increasing modernizing ambitions in the Nordic countries. The role of the state has been exceptionally strong in policies affecting family life and gender relations. Such moulding of intimate relations has been associated with social democracy but applies to most political parties in the period before and after the Second World War. As in the previous century, family reforms were a means to create a society at the forefront of modernity. Science provided a basis on which to build new, rational, and productive citizens. In Sweden, for example, policymakers, experts, and politicians realized that rapid urbanization and industrialization created stress and strain within the family, and sought to address it. Industrialization and urbanization were followed by the rise of the labour movement and early feminism. With a Marxist self-understanding as scientific socialism, social democratic movements were also often acting in tandem with attempts at scientific intervention

Family, gender, and sexuality 39

in all social areas. The family was one of them. Family planning, sex education, and women's rights were on the table. In the 1930s, a sometimes related psychoanalytic movement argued for sexual freedom and alternative forms of family life as ways to fix complex social issues. At the same time, there was great resistance to this kind of radical transformation of the Nordic societies. Conservatives were not convinced that society could be improved in the way, and with the means, suggested by the Social Democrats. They were also at times incensed by the very direction and proposed goals of social development, conflicts that were also addressed in conspiracist Nazi anti-Semitism.

Family and sexuality in Nordic Nazi conspiracy theorizing

The extremely ideological and 'theoretical' nature of Nazi anti-Semitism may have been socially peripheral, but the conspiracy theories of Nordic Nazis expressed broader social and cultural conflicts, albeit from a specific, sectarian point of view.

Few were more ideologically sectarian in their conspiracist anti-Semitism than the former skiing pioneer Halldis Neegaard Østbye (1896–1983). She adopted Nazi ideology very early, and during the 1930s became one of the most prominent Norwegian producers of anti-Semitic propaganda. While her influence outside the fascist party was limited, she was important to their anti-Semitic propaganda. Her own political prominence decreased when, with the German occupation of Norway in 1940, her political party became the Norwegian face of the regime. Her anti-Semitic conspiracy theories, however, continued as part of the party's political messaging – and now her party had power.

Østbye's anti-Semitism included conspiracy theories about 'Jewish-Bolshevik' strategies for destroying the family. Norwegian Nazi ideology at the time differentiated between the overt and the covert influence of the Jewish–Bolshevik conspiracy (de Figueiredo 1994). The attacks on the family belonged to the covert side, so-called *Cultural* Bolshevism. Here, Østbye explained, the evil agents operated on the cultural and scientific arena without showing their true infernal nature to other than discerning individuals. In *The Jews War* (*Jødenes krig*), Østbye (1941) delineates how actors of 'sexual Bolshevism' are undermining true, Aryan morality. The overarching conspiracy theory was, of course imported, but it was adapted to fit local circumstances. Thus the fiends of the story are mixed. Østbye primarily targets non-Nordic Jewish, and allegedly Jewish, doctors, psychoanalysts, and politicians. These are, however, supplemented by prominent Norwegians in social medicine and politics – typically Social Democrats – who are presented as

40   *Family, gender, and sexuality*

adherents of the subversive ideas and policies of Cultural Bolshevism. In the fashion typical of imported, universal conspiracism, the local and the global were fused, with local enemies presented as expression of the global conspiracy. The specific version here, 'sexual Bolshevism', is presented as a road map to 'sexual anarchy' (Østbye 1941: 40) whereby "sexual deviance," such as homosexuality, abortion, and sex work, would be legal. Marriage, on the other hand, would not be legal, and children would be raised communally, deconstructing the notion of family. The goal was presented as twofold: shaping adults in the image of a deviant, oriental, Jewish hypersexuality, and transforming children into 'social marionettes' (Østbye 1941: 44) for a Jewish-Bolshevik society. Against the degenerate nature of oriental and urban hedonism, Østbye presented an ahistorical vision of rural, Nordic bashfulness as the natural consequence of the cold, hard, Nordic climate, leading to a healthier race (de Figueiredo 1994: 91). Good sexual morality was thus a modest one, kept within a heterosexual marriage. The family which needed protection against subversive forces acting on behalf of a more sinister enemy was conservative and patriarchal. Women and men should stick to different roles in society, but Østbye herself was incensed that she was kept away from public politics once the Germans occupied Norway and Nazis were in power.

In the discourse of Østbye we find traces of the nineteenth-century conflict between city and countryside, but it had now developed theoretically. It had been submerged into an ideology, where a mythicized rural society was seen as the truest reflection of the racial character of the Nordic peoples. All the above reflects the selective anti-modernity of Nazi ideology, but although the conspiracist and racialist version was radical, the topics, including culture and gender, were part of the broader debate. As in many things, Østbye took an extreme position, but her conspiracy theories addressed real lines of societal tension. This also includes her anti-Semitism.

Despite the limited presence of Jews in the Nordic countries, anti-Semitic ideation was fairly prevalent. Although the level of propagandistic anti-Semitic ideology was low and rarely developed into fascist or Nazi sympathies, in Nordic as in larger European conspiracy theories, 'race' and 'racial mixture' was a central concern. One anti-Semitic trajectory was agrarianism, in which the pure Nordic and rural race had to be saved from the urban, cosmopolitan, and degenerate influence of the Jews. Another trajectory clustered around extreme nationalism in which the glory of the nation was tied to maintaining the racial purity of the people (see Andersson 2000; Berggren 1999). The majority of the people

Family, gender, and sexuality 41

propagating these ideas were well established and highly educated bourgeois men. This racism – mainly directed against Jews – was infused with typically unspoken gender ideals and gender fears. 'The Jew' was portrayed as effeminate and unmanly, yet simultaneously a dangerous cosmopolitan, luring virtuous Nordic woman to acts of 'race mixture'. Family, gender, and sexuality is central to all racist ideologies, and Nordic anti-Semitism is no exception.

Family, gender, and the state in the post-war period

The Second World War affected all the Nordic countries but in very different ways. The war brought devastation to Finland, and only Sweden and Iceland were untouched by armed conflict. Yet post-war policies in all the Nordic countries were similar, albeit with different economic resources at hand and thus unfolding at different paces. From the late 1940s, better housing, better educational opportunities, new forms of professional childcare, and social service were put forward as a means to help and support families. Welfare policies created a social, political, and economic climate in the Nordic countries where women had a very high degree of participation on the labour market, where maternity – and later paternity – leave increased, and where public childcare became more or less universal.

By the end of the 1970s, however, there emerged experts who were assessing the Nordic welfare policies and the relationship between women, men, and the state more critically. The discourse of consensus underlining the benefits of the Nordic welfare model was questioned by both the political left and right. In the emerging field of gender research, critical voices analyzed the persistence of patriarchy and how women, despite so-called women-friendly policies, 'earned and owned much less than men, had a lower status and less power and took much greater responsibility for childcare and housework' (Lundqvist and Roman 2010: 79). These debates have persisted, and we find them mirrored in Nordic suspicions about secret conspiracies related to gender in the recent past. More period-related research is needed to see how early these topics show up.

Post-war conspiracy culture clearly shows some continuities with the period before. In the early 1950s, scandals in Sweden involving accusations of homosexual prostitution, Nazism, and elite cover-ups led to very polarized public debates. The royal family was implicated by allegedly paying off a blackmailer who claimed he had been sexually involved with the king. In a parallel case, a priest claimed that high-ranking civil servants covered up their involvement in 'homosexual

42 *Family, gender, and sexuality*

rings'. Accusations on the part of well-known Swedish intellectuals demanded that the authorities deal with what was characterized as a 'legal meltdown'. Homosexuality between adults had been legalized in Sweden in 1944, but was not very tolerated. Claims that young boys were being lured into prostitution by criminals were common. The syndicalist paper *Arbetaren* (The Worker) was at the forefront in a campaign accusing elite men, often with Nazi sympathies, of forming a secret Freemason group to sexually abuse young, innocent, working-class men. In contrast to the US debates, homosexuality was not linked to communism, but the tropes were otherwise quite similar, centring on a subversive enemy aiming to infiltrate and conquer society from within (Lennerhed 1994: 86).

Holocaust denial was an early part of far-right post-war conspiracism (see Simonsen 2019), and remnants of the native Nazis regularly engaged in a wide host of conspiracy theories. They still involved Jews and 'communists', but also revolved around family and sexuality. In Norway, the Nazi 'newspaper' *Folk og Land* (People and Land) was one venue for disseminating such narratives. In the 29 June issue in 1968, for instance, the writer 'Munin' rages against all s/he sees as Jewish, from capitalism and communism to Freudian theories of sexuality. The latter segues into cultural criticism where psychoanalysis, as with Østby above, drives promiscuity and a lack of sexual morals, assisted by 'guitar playing monkeys' – specifically popular music in the shape of The Beatles. All were, of course, described as being part of a Jewish plot.

This is also the period where debates over abortion rights became prominent. It became a defining issue both for the left and for Christian Democrats. It most prominently became a central topic dividing the left and more theologically conservative Christians. In Norway, the relations between Labour and revivalist Christianity gradually chilled over differing positions on abortion, family, and gender, and Israel. All of these were later reflected in conspiracy narratives that were partially continuous with pre-war, anti-Communist (and sometimes anti-Semitic) theories, partially centred on new topics and allegations (cf. Færseth 2013). At the time, however, topics of strife were tied less to secret conspiracies than to immoral trends pointing towards the final days. The topics did at times segue into conspiracy speculations, such as in the often apocalyptic, conspiracist writings of Mutter Basilea Schlink (1904–2001).

Schlink was a much-loved German writer and founder of the Evangelical Sisterhood of Mary, whose copious writings on Christian life were rapidly and often translated into most Nordic languages, including Finnish. Her texts centred on devotion and piety, but they

Family, gender, and sexuality   43

were interspersed with references to conspiracy theories about everything from Marxism as a Satanic plot, to the Illuminati, popular music, and the Satanic, licentious nature of modern life. She also raged against abortion, pornography, homosexuality, and blasphemy. These go together, in a conspiracy that is not quite secret, but are still the source that created 'strife between teacher and student, between children and parents, between woman and man' and led to 'increased rebellion, aggression, debauched and perverse sexuality, ruined marriages and families' (Schlink 1976: 70).

Schlink was often published by mainstream Christian publishing houses, but the early, public Nordic reception of her books seems to overlook her conspiracist views. They were submerged in the general cultural criticism, which again got less attention than the calls for piety that both her cultural critique and her conspiracism were part of. Only later did a semi-apocalyptic conspiracism that finds traces of a Satanic 'Illuminati' in all that goes wrong catch on, and then in less mainstream circles.

New family debates: the rights of women, children, and LGBTQ

In the period after the Second World War, debates on sexuality, gender, and family were gradually influenced by migration. After the war, migration influenced all the Nordic countries, but to different degrees. In 1954, the Nordic countries agreed to have open borders and a common labour market. For decades, intra-Nordic labour migration and settlement were the numerically most important, particularly from Finland to Sweden. Migration from the south of Europe and Turkey was substantial until the middle of the 1970s and the economic recession due to the oil crisis. From that period on, migration to the Nordics was instead mainly due to refugees. As will be discussed in the next chapter, this has led to a profound change in the Nordic countries. From the 1980s and especially from the 1990s the Nordic family has become more diverse in terms of national background, religious affiliation, and sexual preferences, as well as varied in reproductive opportunities and choices of parenting. In the same period – and related to this – debates about, and policies towards family, gender, and sexuality in the Nordic countries have become much more fragmented and antagonistic.

In the Nordic countries gender equality, and even feminism, has become a hallmark in national branding. Norway was a pioneer when it came to quotas for women in elections, and Swedish foreign policy is since 2014 said to be feminist. In the last decades, gender equality

44 *Family, gender, and sexuality*

has increasingly been promoted as a specific Nordic national trait, differentiating the 'native' population from, especially, the non-European immigrants with a Muslim background. The tone of voice in this national branding differs from one Nordic country to another (see next chapter). Denmark exhibits much more tolerance for expressions of anti-immigration/anti-Muslim opinions compared to Sweden, but Denmark, Norway, and Sweden have all passed legislation to restrict and combat what is perceived to be patriarchal foreign family arrangements (Hagelund 2008; Rabo 2009; Rytter 2010).

Nordic gender equality has also increasingly come to include official policies to support gay rights and the LGBTQ movement. Marriage is a gender-neutral institution in all Nordic countries. In 2008, Norway was the sixth country in the world to recognize same-sex marriage. Sweden, Iceland, Denmark, and Finland followed. In Finland, however, couples can only be married in a civil service and not in the Lutheran Church.

Not only women but also children became increasingly protected through state policies and law in the Nordic countries. Spanking, and even beating, children as part of their upbringing is common in many societies, but the Nordic countries were from the late 1970s in the forefront of criminalizing such 'family punishment'. Such measures and, from the 1990s, the ratification of the Convention on the Rights of the Child, met with opposition among people with a more traditional and conservative family outlook. Antagonism was typically expressed in terms of opposition to the 'socialist dictatorship'. It also appears, as will be discussed in Chapter 5, in conspiracy theories about the Nordics. Once the discourse on violence against children was seen as effective, moral entrepreneurs put it to broader use (cf. Best 1990). Ever more behaviours were represented as 'violence': physical and emotional neglect, scolding, smoking at home, and other plausibly harmful behaviours were reframed as violence to children. The resulting social problems discourse was closely related to that of violence against women, so that topics related to one were quickly used to focus on 'similar' problems related to the other.

The Satanic conspiracy

During the decades from the 1970s on, several strains of social movements coalesced around questions relating to gender and family. Increased language competencies, international networking, and professionalization of both institutions and non-governmental organizations facilitated the adoption of theories and practices from (primarily)

Family, gender, and sexuality 45

English-speaking countries (cf. Victor 1998). This included conspiracy theories. When first the United States, then Britain were in the grip of Satanic panic, different professional and ideological networks answered to the variety of conspiracy claims within the larger panic. The most elaborated theories claimed that a network of hidden Satanists used popular culture to corrupt children and adolescents, was behind criminal networks relating to everything from small-scale vandalism to drug trafficking and murder, and regularly committed 'Satanic ritual abuse'. The latter often included allegations of ritual sacrifice, and sometimes cannibalism.

Conspiracy beliefs relating to popular culture tapped into earlier, mostly conservative Christian ideas about the corrupting effects of media use and games. There were typically two layers to the claims, with the conspiracy becoming visible in the second, which included supernatural forces. The first layer was an outward-directed, 'secular' discourse. This claimed that Satanists were using areas of popular culture to mislead youth, resulting in mental ill-health, with vandalism, drug use, depression, suicide, and violent crime as a result. Such a discourse was visible in, for example, claims in Denmark in the 1980s that the use of Ouija boards was behind teen suicides.

The claims arose in a specific context (Dyrendal and Lap 2008: 335–340). Early in 1986, the Danish author Erwin Neutzsky-Wulff had gone public with claims that he was part of a Satanic movement which had existed since the 1920s. In widely read interviews, journalists centred on stories that these Satanists recruited and trained 'talented' young men and women in classical languages, the sciences – and magic that could kill by mind alone. The hidden group of Satanists were said to be elite, socially powerful, and to engage their young trainees in sexual behaviour. These stories grabbed public attention. They were consonant with later conspiracy theories, but what unleashed fear at the time was the amalgamation of Neutzsky-Wulff's stories with another, concurrent set of events: a TV film about 'the occult' was said to have led more adolescents to experiment with Ouija boards. Fears about the psychological consequences of such use were already heightened, and Neutzsky-Wulff's stories were inciting religious fervour. Then, one, 18-year-old Ouija practitioner committed suicide.

Stories immediately connected the suicide to Ouija use. The discourse represented the spiritualist experimentation as 'Satanic' and leading to psychological problems and suicide. These claims and fears were disseminated to other Nordic media, to variable interest (Dyrendal and Lap 2008). We see something similar with a related claim involved in Finnish activism. Here heavy metal music and role-playing games

46 *Family, gender, and sexuality*

were presented as a Satanic 'gateway drug', luring the young, then corrupting them further, and leading to violence (Hjelm 2008). For both sets of claims, attention seems to have stayed within circles of those particularly interested as long as there were no relatable, local events to activate panic.

The circle of 'particularly interested' constituted a second, inward-looking, explicitly religious layer of claims. These followed a tradition where youth 'occult' play was understood as literally conducting rituals in order to contact demonic powers (e.g. Dyrendal 2003a). From the traditional, conservative entrepreneurs' point of view, the young had been seduced away from traditional religion and their families, through their use of other, non-Christian narratives and practices to make a sense of self. This concern runs deep within much of the literature, but it was not immediately relevant for those outside devout circles. However, by combining claims about evil actors with harmful psychological and social effects, the propagators of these ideas could mobilize other actors interested in controlling the behaviour of the young: by using a discourse of 'social problems' the claims were placed outside a religious framework, and entrepreneurs could engage a broader public by, for example, making claims fit into larger conspiracy theories about Satanism. Once institutional actors such as therapists, police officers, and youth workers were mobilized, the media played along.

The fears over adolescent pastimes had already tied these to social problems, sometimes in the shape of criminal behaviour. The police and the media were drawn into conspiracy theories about Satanism when they were searching for perpetrators behind, and explanations of, specific, typically minor, criminal episodes. Cemetery vandalism, spraying of graffiti, or vandalism of abandoned houses were interpreted as 'Satanism' in Finland, Denmark, and Norway (Hjelm 2008; Dyrendal and Lap 2008). In circles which had adopted the 'police model' of Satanic crime (see Hicks 1991), this type of crime was seen as a first tier of involvement in the Satanic conspiracy.

The 'police model' developed by US police officers presented a variety of socially deviant adolescent behaviours as parts of a pyramid of Satanic involvement. It was described as a centrally planned journey of degeneracy, inexorably leading to increasing ideological commitment and ideology-consistent criminal activities. Its endpoint was the intergenerational, Satanist cult, where children were brainwashed and controlled through Satanic ritual abuse, and the crimes regularly involved rape and murder, as well as every other sordid behaviour.

This returns us to the cases with which the chapter started, but from another angle. The Swedish cases combined concerns and activism from

Family, gender, and sexuality 47

feminists with allegations of organized crime. It included many of the concerns from the US 'police model', but the latter was highly conservative, particularly with regard to ideas about family and gender. What had happened?

The conspiracy theories about Satanism travelled to the Nordic countries via several, partially independent, networks. Early varieties of conspiracy theories about Satanism were almost exclusively transmitted along conservative Christian networks, and thus contained explicitly evangelizing elements. For example, the watershed publication *Michelle Remembers*, which included an early version of Satanic child abuse revealed through 'recovered memories', presented a rash around her neck as evidence of a 'body memory' of a demonic encounter with Satan's tail. This final part was quietly dropped from later transmission. In the variety of professional networks that got involved, the professions' ideological context determined which elements of the narratives were relevant. Sectarian ideas demanding incongruent ideological frameworks were often dropped, while those that suited preferred frameworks were highlighted.

This reshaped the narratives. Although the ideological background was often still visible, focus shifted to the crimes and other social ills. These could easily be fitted into narratives that suited new actors' interpretations of society. With the rise of sexual abuse claims within the framework of the Satanic conspiracy, the alleged criminal conspiracy came to the attention of feminist ideology and therapy. The addition of claims about ritual crimes against small children in the American and British kindergarten panic drew further networks of professional child protectors into the fray (e.g. Jenkins 1992; Nathan and Snedeker 1995; cf. de Young 2004).

Most of the early networks spreading the conspiracy theory were still highly conservative. Theoretical frameworks from relevant professions, such as the police, psychotherapy, and child welfare, were blended with the existing religious and political ideology in the countries where the conspiracy theories originated. This blending separated out what was salient to give it ideological meaning. The process was repeated in the Nordic countries, and the reception was, of course, dominated by the voices present there, especially in the professional networks and their ideological compatriots (Dyrendal 2003b; 2011). From a feminist point of view, the Satanic conspiracy was the hidden side of the patriarchal order, showing its worst consequences – or patriarchy's 'hidden heart' as one ideologist phrased it (Lundgren 1994). From the conservative side, the decline of 'traditional values', including gender roles, family structure, and modest sexuality, were all part of the interpretation. Thus

48   *Family, gender, and sexuality*

there were two primary ideological takes on very similar conspiracy beliefs, with two very different interpretations of where the problem lay.

However, since the cases that were used as evidence to illustrate the conspiracy theories were inevitably connected to allegations of crime, the police and the judicial system tended to become involved. Before reaching that stage, the cases could have other origins: psychotherapy in the case of 'adult survivors', and child protection and social workers in the case of children. Unlike in the United Kingdom, child protection services were more likely to be connected to women's shelters and feminist groups, thus several of the cases that started as suspicion about sexual or physical abuse were disseminated and interpreted within a feminist framework. This meant that the cases came with a demand for belief in the victim's narrative, derived from campaigns against rape. The therapist's reconstruction or the social worker's tale became, as with the international material, a substitute for original testimony by alleged victims. This meant the conspiracy belief could spread rapidly through the networks (cf. LaFontaine 1998). They did, however, meet both internal resistance and external opposition, especially after the first wave of claims had been investigated and dropped.

The external opposition is more interesting for our purpose here. When conspiracy theories enter the public arena, they are generally opposed, and the language of opposition is typically that of a critical, rational weighing of evidence, often combined with ridicule. In the case of the Satanism scare, the ridicule was mostly reserved for claims regarding popular culture. The claims of serious crime, involving the police, the judicial system, and multiple sets of academic and clinical 'experts', were instead framed as a struggle over the future of society. The discourse of 'rationality' was opposed to that of blind faith, and it was often combined with a conservative sociopolitical stance. Both Christian and feminist narratives were invoking civilizational crisis in the shape of Satanic conspiracy; thus, the mere act of denying the crisis served as a defence of the status quo. However, the 'rationality' stance was also used in a crisis mode of its own. By invoking a rhetoric of the other's anti-rationality, it was presenting a rational society under attack by fanatical extremists. This framing was also used by activists who saw the Satanic conspiracy beliefs of radical feminists as the logical conclusion of feminist ideology. Such radical beliefs were thus simultaneously a threat to conventional marriage, the nuclear family, reason, and due process.

Men's rights activists and conservative families in conflict with child protection services were among those who made active use of the controversy. Media coverage and interest in the conspiracy theories about

Family, gender, and sexuality 49

Satanism died down, but, in one sense, the front lines hardened as the terrain shifted. The lines of conflict had always played out on the terrain of victim's rights. However, since there were claims of violent crime on the one hand and claims of false accusations on the other – with 'evidence' being slippery at best – the public struggle over truth became a contest over who the real victims were and how they were victimized. This part of the sociocultural reception of the controversy over bad therapy, false memories, conspiracy theories, and dubious judicial processes were then included in anti-feminist conspiracy beliefs. Paradoxically, they included parts of the original conspiracy claims. During the 2000s and later, opposition towards Norwegian child protection services incorporated accusations that children were kidnapped by the services to make use of them in paedophile rings. Sometimes these accusations also contained the Satanic conspiracy. This is discussed more in detail in Chapter 5.

Nordic exceptionalism revisited

The Nordic countries have followed a global trend where identity politics is intimately connected to family, gender, and sexual politics. Identity politics is displayed and performed on a battleground in which ideological boundaries and conspiracy theories criss-cross in different, complex, and shifting ways. The embrace of queer politics and gay rights has created a boundary, especially against non-Nordic outsiders who oppose them. This nativist rhetoric tends to include 'concerns' about women's rights. But there is also an increasing, extreme anti-feminism that comes from both similar and other circles. Mostly outside the nativist rhetoric, various versions of fathers' rights movements have developed in all Nordic countries since the 1970s. Their aim was often to change family laws and policies perceived to be skewed against fathers. But in the last decade these movements feature much more militant and extreme right-wing voices, which simultaneously spew hate about gays, Muslim (and non-Western) immigrants – and feminists. The most infamous case is, of course, Anders Behring Breivik, described in the next chapter. In his so-called manifesto, women are singled out as traitors if they marry or have children with non-Nordic men, and feminism is presented as part of the 'cultural-Marxist' conspiracy. In the classical far-right combination of hostile sexism (women are inferior, emotional, manipulative etc.) and 'benevolent' sexism (women are 'the fairer sex' and should be protected etc.), the true role of women is to be mother to Nordic children, with men as heroic, masculine protectors. Feminism and cultural Marxism are seen to invert the role, invoking

50 *Family, gender, and sexuality*

solely hostile sexism. While his case is extreme and overtly conspiracist, the anti-feminist venom on the Internet has increasingly become normalized (Sveland 2013).

One case where conspiracy theories moved from the margins of social media to the mainstream concerns the Swedish Academy. In 2016, the royal Swedish institution awarding the prestigious Nobel Prize for Literature was caught in the middle of a scandal that involved nepotism, sexual harassment, and shady financial compensation. In the wake of the international #MeToo movement, 18 women stepped forward and accused Jean-Claude Arnault, linked to the academy through his wife, writer Katarina Frostensson, of sexual abuse. It then emerged that the academy had been alerted to Arnault's behaviour two decades earlier, but had continued to sponsor a cultural venue run by him and his wife, and had also informally granted him extensive privileges. In 2018, Arnault was sentenced to prison for rape. Both before and after the trial, a group of Danish and Swedish journalists and academics accused the 18 women and the Swedish newspaper *Dagens Nyheter* of orchestrating a sinister, postmodern, cultural Marxist, and feminist plot against one of the last bastions of 'The Enlightenment'. One Swedish journalist argued (Wong 2018) that the Swedish public had been manipulated to destroy the reputation of Arnault and his protectors. For another Swedish journalist, Lena Anderson, the attacks on the academy implied the collapse of the liberal cultural nation of Sweden as we know it. Arnault was only targeted and scapegoated out of envy and populist contempt, she argued. Her article was illustrated with an image of the Bastille, representing the Swedish Academy, and a manic crowd of people with pitchforks, torches, and sticks. Moreover, Anderson claimed that

> a cult has been created around these eighteen women we now are asked to sacrifice to – and we don't know what the final price will be. Exactly as in other cults you don't know when you have paid off this, this guilt and who is guilty.
>
> (Anderson 2018)

The most far-reaching accusations have been made by Danish writer Marianne Stidsen (2018). She accused those critical of the Swedish Academy as fomenting a left-wing, populist, totalitarian revolution under the banner of identity politics. The values of true and false, right and wrong were perverted to serve a goal driven by 'blind bloodthirstiness' (Stidsen 2018). She likened the feminists critiquing the Swedish Academy to the Taliban and insisted that the progress of the last two centuries now risked a complete Armageddon.

Family, gender, and sexuality 51

Arnault was convicted and the Swedish Academy was forced to begin a painful transformation. But there are no signs that conspiracy theories targeting those critical of the Swedish Academy have diminished. Instead they are more entrenched. Stidsen inscribes herself into a tradition in Sweden's neighbouring countries in which Swedish policy failures are increasingly described as the outcome of a delusional, vast, and misguided government conspiracy.

Gender research is one such target in contemporary conspiracist writing. In December 2018, for example, a suspected bomb was found on the premises of the National Secretariat for Gender Studies in Göteborg, Sweden. This was not the first time threats were made against that institution or against gender research in general. Again, the motivating force and resulting rhetoric is only partially home grown. Lena Martinsson, a professor of gender studies in Göteborg, has studied how anti-feminist rhetoric from predominantly Catholic countries has travelled to the Nordic countries. Arriving here, gender research is depicted as an overarching and dominant ideology which threatens the modern and rational society and our universities. Her research on different anti-gender movement shows that they are united by their claims of a gender ideology undermining important values and conspiring to take over the world. In an interview in the journal for the university teachers' union, she stresses that gender research has always been under fire, but now the attack is part of a transnational movement (Skarsgård 2019: 24).

Some of this movement's ideas are explicitly conspiracist, and while some target 'globalists', some Islam, and others feminism (or women in general), there is considerable overlap. Conspiracist imaginations about these actors are not found solely in extremist circles, but it is there that the combination is most elaborately developed. Breivik's so-called manifesto is a relevant example: the enemy outside, Islam, is construed as fundamentally different and destructive. Islam and Muslims are identified as the dangerous outsiders who threaten fundamental European values, but his real targets are the 'cultural Marxists' – the enemy within. The 'manifesto' is conspiracist throughout, in varying degrees, depending on who Breivik decided to copy-paste. Sometimes it is filled with a nostalgia that not merely recalls Halldis Neegard Østbye's anger towards 'sexual Bolshevism'; it also refers to the same sources of its cultural illness. Feminism, for its part, is a totalitarian ideology that is aligned with not merely cultural Marxism, but also the Muslim invaders, while it turns Western man into 'a touchy-feely subspecies' (p.37). The programme of emasculation and destruction of families goes together with a globalist, multiculturalist agenda to destroy all nations and their characteristics (e.g. p. 709). Thus the conspiracy is seen to deconstruct

52 *Family, gender, and sexuality*

the larger family of European and national culture with the nuclear family, masculinity, and proper sexual morality.

Some of the specific sources were Nordic. Ideas about gender, family, and sexuality have been used as part of national branding. But as discussed in this chapter the sentiments and arguments are also copied from international discussions. The Nordic conspiracy discourse on family, gender, and sexuality is thoroughly internationalized, and in its later phases, gender roles and family are threatened by internal dissent, but also by the dangerous outsiders we consider more closely in the next chapter.

4 Migration and the dangerous outsiders

Anti-immigrant conspiracy theories in the Nordic countries

The terrorist attack in Norway on 22 July 2011 was the most horrible incident of Nordic extreme nationalism in contemporary times. A lone wolf attacker, Anders Behring Breivik massacred 77 people, mainly young members of the Labour Party, gathered on a small island close to Oslo (Bergmann 2018; Önnerfors 2017a: 159–175). In a lengthy and largely incoherent document he posted online prior to the attack, he had gathered articles, blog posts and other items from far-right sources that argued that Europe was being ruined by the influx of Muslim immigrants and that the continent was culturally under siege by foreign infiltrators. He accused mainly feminists and the social democratic elite of having betrayed the European public.

Anders Breivik was a believer in the so-called Eurabia conspiracy theory, which is one of the most prominent theories about dangerous outsiders in contemporary times, and refers to the fear of Muslims replacing the Christian population with Islam. The Eurabia theory can be viewed as a subset of the overall Great Replacement theory. In 2011, a deeply controversial French philosopher, Renaud Camus, titled his book *The Great Replacement*. Camus argued that French (and European) civilization and identity were at risk of being subsumed by mass migration, especially from Muslim-dominated countries, and because of low birth rates among the native French people. Numerous nativist populist leaders in Europe have promoted this theory, nurturing the myth that migrants – especially Muslims – were taking over our national soil and heritage (Bergmann 2020).

Anders Breivik adopted the position that the EU was a project to turn the continent culturally into Eurabia, insisting that Muslims, aided by domestic elites in Europe, were plotting to turn the continent into an Islamic society. He accused his victims in the Norwegian Labour Party of being cultural Marxists responsible for ruining his country's Nordic heritage with their feminist and multicultural beliefs.

54 *Migration and the dangerous outsiders*

This horrible terrorist attack in Norway was just one example of the effects that extreme right-wing conspiracy theorists can have on some of the more unstable recipients of their messages. Studies have found that conspiracy theories can be a catalyst for extremism (van Prooijen et al. 2015). Bartlett and Miller (2010) indicated that conspiracy theories played a role in all extremist groups they examined who were engaged in terrorism and political violence. In other words, conspiracy theories can pose a serious threat to public order in democratic societies, but some theories reach further into political mainstreams than merely to the realm of violent extremists. In this chapter we examine those conspiracy theories in the Nordic countries that centre on migration and the ideas of dangerous others.

Early anti-Semitism

Nordic discourse on dangerous outsiders is, of course, not new, nor is it specifically Nordic. Causes, concerns, and tropes have often been acquired and borrowed from larger circles of European thinkers. While conspiracy theories about 'outsiders' may be associated with extremism, promoters of such theories have not always been considered marginal or extreme. For centuries Jews, for example, have often been framed as 'others', in opposition to 'proper' native citizens. They were construed as a secretive and conspiratorial 'state within the state', suspected of disguising as insiders, without really fitting in with the domestic population.

This attitude was expressed clearly in the discussions on the Norwegian constitution of 1814, where county judge Lauritz Weidemann (1775–1856) brought a draft which said that Jews should be excluded, because they were insurgents and prone to fraud and conspiracy. Their religion would, moreover, always motivate them to seek separate statehood and intrigue, making them inclined to create a 'state within the state' (Ulvund 2017: 59). The trope originated in larger established European debates, starting in absolutist monarchy as a slogan against those encroaching on the sovereign's power (52f.). It soon developed into an antirepublican slogan and was effectively transformed to also target minorities like the Jews, emphasizing their threat from within. What had been a matter of debate about Jews a few decades earlier had by the early 19th Century become 'common knowledge' (59). Until 1851 Jews were constitutionally denied entry into Norway.

The discourse on Jews as a particular conspiratorial threat had been building over a long period of time. They were suspected of bypassing the sovereign authority by taking on an internal state-like role. Similar

Migration and the dangerous outsiders 55

suspicions were also afloat regarding other groups, such as Jesuits, Freemasons, Huguenots, the military, and the aristocracy, who were all also suspected of effectively forming a 'state within the state' (Ulvund 2017: 49).

Criticism of the aristocracy as a parasitic organism on productive society was easily conflated with anti-Semitism. In wake of the French Revolution, and related to local Nordic economic crises, anti-Semitism was unleashed with ferocious power in Denmark and Sweden in 1813 and 1815. This was but one of many episodes, resulting in depicting Jews as parasites in society. They were presented as unmodern and uncivilized; cowardly, not courageous; lecherous, not moral; lazy, rather than industrious; egotistic, rather than selfless (Ulvund 2017: 64f.) – thus, not fit to be real citizens.

Nation-state formation occurred relatively late in the Nordic countries. The Swedish–Norwegian union was dissolved in 1905, and in 1918 Finland escaped from under Russia while Iceland won sovereignty from Denmark. This period saw a renewed emphasis on defining and preserving each of the distinct national cultures, while also elevating ideas about 'dangerous others'. These ideas about 'us' and 'others' were shaped by broader currents of biological racism and theories of 'national characteristics' (cf. Mosse 1964).

In Sweden, racial ideology was established early through the State Institute for Racial Biology (1922). In a spirit of social Darwinism and Cesare Lombroso's criminal anthropology, the Swedish people were studied, and collective characteristics were ascribed to regional collectives, ethnic minorities, and 'outsiders' alike. Thus, a clear narrative could be detected about who belonged to the pristine national community and who were excluded from it. In Finland, the victory of the 'Whites' in the civil war following the Russian Revolution promoted ideas of 'Jewish Bolshevism'. Communism was seen as a Jewish plot to subdue national sentiment and the pride of the Finnish people (Elmgren 2018: 9–32). These positions kept anti-Semitism thriving until Finland entered the Second World War on the side of Nazi Germany.

Although Nazi anti-Semitism was extremely racist and conspiracist, negative attitudes against Jews were much more widespread than that. In Denmark, the cultural opposition to the leading liberal (and Jewish) intellectual Georg Brandes drew on Édouard Drumont's anti-Semitic and conspiracist *La France Juive* (1886) in placing him as an outsider. With the influx of Russian emigrés after the revolution, the Nordic countries were introduced to the *Protocols of the Elders of Zion*. The combination of critique of modernity's ills with conspiracist explanations spurred agrarian populists to take an authoritarian turn. Those kinds

56 *Migration and the dangerous outsiders*

of anti-Semitic tropes were then marginalized by the notorieties of Nazi Germany.

After the war, a renewed wave of anti-Semitism rose, for example, in Sweden, with the influx of Jewish refugees, who were often discussed in apocalyptic terms and their integration into the Swedish labour market heavily contested.

Anti-immigration

In the post-war era, both Denmark and Sweden gained a reputation for being open, liberal, and tolerant. During a period of economic boom, an influx of foreign workers, mainly from northern Africa, Turkey, and the Balkans arrived in the 1960s, followed by increasing numbers of (political) refugees from, for example, South America and the Middle East. Their numbers were significantly lower in Finland, Iceland, and Norway. In Sweden, a relatively migration-friendly policy and tolerance towards migrants and refugees was initially deemed an integral part of its social liberalism, and multiculturalism fitted neatly into the Swedish national identity.

In Denmark, the discourse on immigration, however, changed drastically in the 1970s and 1980s, from emphasizing equal treatment and protecting human rights to the requirement to adhere to the fundamental values of the Danish society. Nationalism was reawakening and soon immigrants and refugees were, through a culturally based neoracist rhetoric, discursively constructed as a threat to Danish national identity and values. These developments in the domestic discourse evolved much later and to a lesser extent in the other Nordics.

Danish politics took a lasting turn in the so-called Earthquake Elections of 1973. With a new political party, the Progress Party, controversial tax attorney Mogens Glistrup rushed onto the scene with a strong anti-tax rhetoric, waging an all-out political attack on the mainstream, which he claimed was burdening the ordinary man beyond what the public could tolerate. Denmark was at a political juncture. Fatigue with the established parties was growing and nationalism was reawakening, and, as Karen Wren (2001) maintains, cultural racism was on the rise. Wren posits that Denmark has since proved especially fertile for cultural racism, turning fundamentally intolerant in the 1980s. She concludes that, paradoxically, the former liberal values in Denmark were used to legitimate negative representation of others, especially Muslims and refugees, who were being framed in the national discourse as a threat to Danish national identity. As an illustration of this, Mogens Glistrup compared Muslim immigrants to a 'drop of arsenic in

Migration and the dangerous outsiders 57

a glass of clear water' (qtd. in Wren 2001: 155). Once this turning point in perception of the 'other' occurred, the next step was to connect it to narratives of conspiracy, which identified internal and external enemies plotting against the interests of the Danish people. It can be difficult to pinpoint exactly when this occurred, but Denmark had been struck by Eurosceptic sentiment, leading to a referendum in 1992 in which further European integration was rejected and instead opt-outs were agreed in the following year. As in the case of the Swedish EU referendum in 1994, Euroscepticism voiced in Scandinavia during the 1990s painted the EU as a manipulative and oppressive super-state or even a secret agent of Catholicism. Whereas a clear nexus is difficult to establish, the subsequent narrative of a 'Eurabian' conspiracy fused anti-EU 'elite critique' with more aggressive Islamophobic positions.

The Danish Progress Party was instrumental in the process of externalizing immigrants and in portraying Denmark as being overrun by foreigners. In the early 1980s, the party became increasingly anti-immigrant, especially in response to the influx of refugees from the Iraq–Iran war. It was coming close to fully adopting the winning formula of many populist parties – that of combining right-wing politics with a policy of anti-immigration (Kitschelt and McGann 1997).

In Norway, right-wing populist Anders Lange set out to mirror Glistrup's success. Lange was linked to nationalist movements of the interwar years, such as the quasi-fascist Fatherland League. Similar to his Danish counterpart, however, it was his emphasis on breaking up the tax system and claiming to stand up for the ordinary man against the elite that appealed to the public. Lange was a controversial but charismatic figure, as evidenced by his aggressive TV presence, where he would often use cruel humour to mock his political establishment rivals, much to the amusement of his audience (Widfeldt 2015).

In 1978, Lange's successor in parliament, Carl I. Hagen, rose to the helm. Influenced by Glistrup's party in Denmark, Anders Lange's Party had been rebranded into the Fremskrittspartiet (FrP, Norway's 'Progress Party'). Hagen was one of the earliest established politicians in Norway to make use of conspiracy theory in a climate of hardened anti-immigrant rhetoric.

In the 1987 election campaign, he quoted a letter that he falsely claimed to have received from a Muslim called Mustafa. The 'letter' effectively described a conspiracy of Muslim immigrants planning to take over Norway. This was quite remarkable as Muslims accounted for only a very small fraction of the population. Still, he did not hesitate to press a conspiracy narrative that was effectively an early version of the Great Replacement conspiracy theory (cf. Zuquete 2018). Although the

58　*Migration and the dangerous outsiders*

letter proved to be his own fabrication, in fact a full-fledged political forgery, that did not hurt the FrP, which won 12.3% of the vote – mainly on the anti-immigrant platform.

With regard to Finland, the number of Allophones – speakers of non-regional languages – only started to rise from the early 1990s, and then from a very low level. Since then, numbers have risen to around 7% of the population. Since the Finnish category of 'immigrants' is reported to be 'highly racialized and class-based' (Leinonen 2012: 213), it is likely that this gave rise to an increased conspiracist discourse on foreigners. The topic did not, however, get research attention or gain real political traction until much later.

Into the mainstream

By the turn of the twenty-first century, Pia Kjærsgaard had replaced Mogens Glistrup as the most influential neo-nationalist in Denmark, when establishing her Danish People's Party (DF) with several members who had left the Progress Party in 1995. The terrorist attacks in the United States on 11 September 2001 brought new support for the DF. Prior to that, most in the mainstream of Danish politics had consistently and firmly opposed its anti-Muslim politics and the party was harshly criticized for flirting with racism. That drastically changed after 9/11. Similar to the significance of the 1973 Earthquake Elections, the 2001 election broke new ground in Danish politics. Firstly, the DF was gaining legitimacy and would henceforth be considered a permanent party in Danish politics. Secondly, immigration rose to become perhaps the most salient issue in the country's political debate.

For many, the terrorist attacks served to validate the DF's criticism of Islam (Widfeldt 2015). Mogens Camre, a DF representative in the EU Parliament, tapped directly into the Great Replacement conspiracy theory when describing Islam as an 'ideology of evil' and suggesting that Muslims should be 'driven out of Western civilization' (qtd. in Klein 2013). He maintained that Muslims couldn't successfully be integrated into Danish society, and he said that they had indeed come to take over Denmark. Adhering to the Eurabia conspiracy theory, Camre said that all Western countries had been 'infiltrated by Muslims', and that even though many of them 'spoke nicely to us, they are waiting to become numerous enough to get rid of us' (qtd. in Sommer and Aagaard 2003). In the wake of the terrorist attacks, the election campaign came to revolve around immigration and the DF surged.

Many of the mainstream parties started to follow the DF's line on immigration, and a relatively widespread consensus emerged on the

Migration and the dangerous outsiders   59

need to stem migration and impose stricter demands on foreigners to integrate and adhere to the Danish way of life. The DF skilfully rode the rise in anti-Muslim sentiment that was enhanced by 9/11. Their anti-immigration rhetoric revolved around three main themes: cultural infiltration, criminality, and welfare abuse. In the 2011 election campaign, a party poster asked: 'Your Denmark? A multi-ethnic society with gang rapes, repression of women and gang crimes. Do you want that?' (see Klein, 2013). The party's new position of power was cemented in 2001 when it backed a minority government of the right-of-centre Venstre and the Conservative Party led by Anders Fogh Rasmussen.

Norwegian scholar Anders Jupskås (2015a) found the DF to be especially successful in linking other political issues to immigration, such as welfare, the state of the economy, and anti-elitism. Immigration was also directly linked to gender issues. DF representatives, for example, maintained that Islam was incompatible with the level of gender equality in Denmark. The veiling of women in Islam became a central and symbolic issue, and the DF was able to set the agenda for the elections.

The DF's 2002 principal manifesto described immigrants as parasites on the Danish welfare system. The party's youth movement went further down a conspiratorial path. In 2003 their advertisements linked Muslims with mass rapes and gang criminality (Widfeldt 2015). Gradually, the DF's rhetoric became the dominant political discourse on migration and Muslims in the country. When arguing that cultural racism had found especially fertile territory in Denmark, Karen Wren (2001) maintains that the absence of significant counter-rhetoric has also become institutional and part of the very fabric of Danish society.

Although populist politics started out on a similar platform in Norway as they had done in Denmark, FrP evolved to become a much milder version of their Danish counterpart. Still, the two evolved in a similar direction. Anniken Hagelund (2003) explains how the FrP moved from problematizing migration merely on economic grounds to also voicing concerns about its effect on Norway's culture. Ever since, the party has argued that in order to prevent ethnic conflict in Norway, immigration and asylum sought from 'outside the Western culture complex' had to be stemmed.[1] This was a classic nationalist ethno-pluralist doctrine, emphasizing the importance of keeping nations separate without openly claiming any sort of superiority.

Carl I. Hagen argued that non-Western immigration would bring a culture of violence and a gang mentality to Norway. Concerns over its effect on the ethnic composition of the nation were increasingly voiced, often quoting former Conservative Prime Minister Kaare Willoch, who

60 *Migration and the dangerous outsiders*

had warned against 'too rapid changes in the unified character of our population' (qtd. in Hagelund 2003).

While the FrP firmly refused to be associated with racism, their representatives positioned themselves as brave truth-tellers, defying the political correctness of the mainstream ruling class. In 2005, for example, the party published a poster depicting a juvenile of foreign descent pointing a gun at the viewer. Its text read: 'The perpetrator is of foreign origin'. When criticized for its xenophobic tone, the party spokesman said that it was simply necessary to 'call a spade a spade' (Jupskås 2015b).

The anti-immigrant position of the FrP was based on a new narrative in which immigrants were presented as an economic burden and a cultural threat rather than being biologically inferior (Rydgren 2007). Anders Hellström (2016) documents how the immigration issue gained prominence in the party's repertoire in the 1990s when warning against the danger of cultural heterogeneity; the immigration issue was in that way 'transformed from an economic to a cultural issue'.

Anders Jupskås (2015b) identifies five distinctive narratives that defined the anti-immigration platform of the FrP. First, that immigrants cost too much. Second, that they exploit 'our' welfare. Third, that they are more prone to crime than the native population. Fourth, that they undermine the Norwegian way of life. And lastly, that they challenge Norway's mainly liberal values. Thus, when combined, they threaten Norway's economy, welfare system, security, culture, and liberal values.

While the narratives may be distinctive, they are highly interrelated and, collectively, they can be combined to craft powerful conspiracy theories against newcomers. In a 2017 survey conducted by the Norwegian Holocaust Centre, negative stereotypes about Muslims in general correlate highly with the conspiracy belief that Muslims aspire to take over Europe. These prejudiced opinions combine to form a working conspiracy stereotype about Muslims, and they predict attitudes that 'we' cannot afford to take in refugees, as well as support for violence (Dyrendal 2020).

Jupskås documents that the first two narratives were present from the outset, that the second two narratives emerged in the 1980s, but that the last one, which challenged liberal values, was only presented after 9/11. In any event, it is clear that the cultural emphasis in the anti-immigrant rhetoric, that is, on rules, norms, and values, only came to prominence in Norway in the 1990s. Simultaneously, the importance of the economic frameworks gradually decreased.

The anti-immigration rhetoric of the Norwegian FrP gradually grew more distinctly anti-Muslim. In 1979, Carl I. Hagen described Islam

Migration and the dangerous outsiders 61

as a 'misanthropic and extremely dangerous religion' (qtd. in Jupskås 2013). Since then, the anti-Islam rhetoric of the party became more insistent. Muslim immigration was linked to terrorism, forced marriage, and crime (Bergmann 2017). Muslim immigrants were portrayed as a burden on the welfare system and as a threat to Norway's culture. The FrP furthermore identified a need to fight against sharia law being implemented in Muslim areas in Norway.

Anti-foreign

On an ethno-nationalist premise, the Danish People's Party sought to shield Denmark from foreign influence accompanying migration. Their 2009 party manifesto concluded that a multicultural society was destined to be 'without inner context and cohesion', and that it was 'burdened by lack of solidarity', and, thus, 'prone to conflict' (qtd. in Widfeldt 2015). The presence of ethnic minorities in Denmark is here discursively problematized and presented as a threat to a fragile homogeneous Danish culture. Karen Wren (2001) described this depiction in Denmark as 'a historically rooted set of traditions now under threat from globalization, the EU, and from "alien" cultures'.

After a decade in a position of power, the DF was able to push through perhaps the strictest immigration laws in the Western world. This shift had become evident during the 2011 general election debate. The DF's polarizing division between 'us' and 'them' had by then evolved to become a shared understanding in the immigrant debate across the political spectrum (Boréus, 2010).

Throughout the process of acquiring mainstream acceptance, the DF firmly kept up its anti-immigrant rhetoric. That was illustrated in the following two examples: In a TV debate in November 2010, Pia Kjærsgaard suggested banning satellite dishes in immigrants' 'ghettos', because they were ugly and because through them Muslims in Denmark gained access to Arabic TV channels such as Al-Jazeera and Al Arabiya (Klein 2013). In the wake of the Paris terrorist attack in late 2015, where Muslim jihadists, mainly from Belgium and France, killed 129 people, the DF's foreign policy spokesman, Søren Espersen, said in a TV interview that Western military forces should now start bombing civil targets in Syria, specifically also in areas where there were women and children (Espersen 2015).

As has been illustrated, the DF was successfully transformed from obscurity to become one of the most influential parties in Danish politics. Interestingly, it did this by changing the political discourse in Denmark on immigration and Islam rather than by altering much its

62 *Migration and the dangerous outsiders*

own often conspiratorial message, such as when adhering to the Eurabia theory. In the new millennium, the once condemned policies of the DF had become not only fully normalized but also much more widely supported in society.

Frustrated by seeing their support bleed over to the Danish People's Party, the Social Democrats – the once hegemonic power in Danish politics – started to follow in the direction of the DF. During the 2015 general election the then-Social Democratic leader, Helle Thorning-Schmidt, embarked on a campaign where she advocated for imposing stricter rules on asylum seekers, and for imposing tighter demands on immigrants to adhere to Danish values.

A much more significant shift, though, occurred after Mette Frederiksen assumed power in the party in 2015. With Frederiksen at the helm, the Social Democrats took several steps further to abandon their former opposition to the DF's policies on immigration. Instead, the party more or less accepted the strict immigration policy, and, largely, made it their own.

The story of the DF's impact on the Social Democrats in Denmark is interesting for understanding the dynamics between populist and mainstream parties. In the so-called Paradigm Shift legislation of 2019, the Social Democrats even came to support the right-wing government's increased restrictions on immigrants. The band of measures included, for example, a ban on wearing burqas and increased repatriation of refugees out of Denmark. By that time, Denmark had already been all but closed to refugees. In only a few decades, the debate in Denmark had shifted from the issue of accepting migrants to the question of expelling them from the country.

In 2019 the DF was falling victim to its own success, when its support was cut by more than half in the general election. The downfall was primarily caused by the Social Democrats closing in on their space, effectively by copying their policies. But the DF was also squeezed from the more extreme right. Two new parties, New Right (*Nye Borgerlige*) and Hard Line (*Stram Kurs*), emerged with calls to expel most Muslims from the country. Nye Borgerlige, the more moderate of the two, garnered 2.4%, or just over 83,000 votes, netting them four seats in Parliament on a law-and-order platform of traditional conservatism promising to 'send home' criminal Muslims after the first offence and to ban traditional Muslim headwear in public. Further to the right, Stram Kurs obtained 1.8% of the vote with just over 63,000 votes, which made it the largest party not to enter Parliament (Kosiara-Pedersen 2020: 1015).

Hard Line is centred around Rasmus Paludan, a lawyer who became famous (or infamous) via his YouTube videos in which he burned

Migration and the dangerous outsiders 63

the Koran in Muslim-majority neighbourhoods while engaging in profanity-laden tirades with the local residents. Paludan's controversial events all took place under the strictest police protection, referring to the safeguarding of his freedom of speech (Ringberg and Kristiansen 2019). Hard Line (and to a lesser degree New Right) adheres to the Great Replacement and Eurabia conspiracy theories, which helps explain the party's desire to expel most Muslims from Denmark.

Even though the DF massively lost support in the 2019 election, its politics were still the greater winner. In fact, previously fringe political positions had become mainstream in Danish politics – and the acceptance of a tough stance on immigration helped pave the way for far-right parties with even tougher platforms on immigration to enter political life. The adherence to and communication of anti-Muslim conspiracy theories by the DF, New Right, and Hard Line has made these theories a more visible and accepted facet of Danish political culture.

Further north, immigration had also become the issue most discussed by Progress Party representatives in Norway, mentioned twice more often, before the 2009 election, than healthcare, the next most frequent topic discussed (Jupskås 2013). Siv Jensen, who had succeeded Carl I. Hagen in 2006 as party leader, warned against what she referred to as 'sneak Islamisation'. This notion alludes to a hidden conspiracy already in motion, which eventually would alter Norway and turn it away from its liberal Christian roots and towards becoming a society based on Islam. In flirting with the Eurabia conspiracy theory, Siv Jensen maintained that the demands of the Muslim community, such as halal meat being served in schools, the right to wear hijab, and the right of public celebration of Muslim holidays, were all examples of the process she called 'sneak Islamisation' (qtd. in Jupskås 2015). In the election campaign, the very term came to define the party's bid to the Norwegian people.

Dog whistle rhetoric and extremism

Although Norwegian populists in parliament have been of the milder kind compared to similar parties elsewhere, the country has still seen its fair share or violent far-right extremism, as was evident in the horrible terrorist attack by Anders Behring Breivik, discussed at the beginning of this chapter. Breivik had previously belonged to the FrP, but he failed to find within it much success, which caused him to abandon the party.

The Breivik attack still caused the FrP grave difficulty. His former involvement threatened its hard-earned legitimacy. The party leadership campaigned vigorously to disown him and instantly toned down its

64 *Migration and the dangerous outsiders*

anti-Muslim rhetoric. For that, Pia Kjærsgaard of the Danish People's Party was critical and said that Siv Jensen was 'lacking spine' (qtd. in Skarvoy and Svendsen 2011).

The setback proved only to be temporary. Two years later the party had won back much of their former support and entered government as a junior partner in a minority coalition with the Conservative Party. In addition to the FrP moving further into the mainstream, it has also been documented how the two most influential mainstream parties in Norway, the Labour Party and the Conservative Party, gradually followed the same path in the debate on immigration and came to adopt much of its rhetoric (Simonnes 2011).

The Breivik attack shed light on a mostly overlooked subculture of Islamophobia and racism in Norway. A network of racist and Islamophobic groupuscules were operating online and around the country. Their venues, like the groups themselves, were mostly extremely marginal, but some were also active on more popular platforms. One of these larger forums was *document.no*, a platform that included 'alternative news' focusing on immigration and on problematizing Islam. In their comments section, Norwegian racists actively engaged in promoting their views.

Breivik's main hero, Fjordman, had been an active commenter on the platform. This 'dark prophet of Norway' as he was called, was a blogger who mostly wrote for international venues (e.g. *Gates of Vienna*), where he predicted that native Norwegians would soon be in the minority if the political elite were allowed to continue destroying European culture and turn the continent into a 'Eurabia'. Breivik responded with a call to all cultural conservatives to defy the demographic infiltration of Muslims and proposed a goal to expel all Muslims from Norway (Seierstad 2015).

Breivik's terrorist act was met with calls for open dialogue and mass demonstrations where people carried a rose – the symbol of the Labour Party, whose youth had been murdered, and a common memorial flower. The elegant and calm response drew some criticism. American expat Bruce Bawer, an influential critic of a welfare-orientated and social-liberal Norway, wrote a book criticizing the social liberal left for using the terrorist act as a tool to silence the debate about Islam. He went so far as to argue that Labour Party supporters were the new Quislings of Norway (Bawer 2012).

Numerous other far-right movements have existed in Norway. Coinciding with the hardened anti-immigration rhetoric of the FrP in the late 1980s, several militant movements grew. These marginal groups included, for example, the White Alliance (Hvit Valgallianse)

Migration and the dangerous outsiders   65

and the People's Movement Against Immigration (Folkebevegelsen mot innvandring). The neo-Nazi group Boot Boys were able to maintain activity in parts of eastern Oslo, parading the streets and violently attacking immigrants, mainly refugees from North Africa and the Middle East.

Like in most places, biological racism was rarely in the open in Norway in the post-war era. Public versions of racist views had surely and squarely moved away from being based on biology towards being based on culture. However, such examples still existed, and were even evident at the time of the Breivik trial, for instance, when Roma people set up camp in Oslo. The camp suffered numerous attacks, and its inhabitants were described as 'rats' and 'inhuman' (see Booth 2014).

An interesting example of the dog-whistle racism that FrP members often applied in election campaigns came before the September 2017 parliamentary election. For several days leading up to the vote, Norway's integration minister for the FrP, Sylvi Lishaug, was able to make almost the entire political debate revolve around her planned visit to neighbouring Sweden, to the Stockholm suburb of Rinkeby. Seeing support fall ahead of the election, after her party had entered government four years earlier, Listhaug played the one card that was most likely to turn the tide for her party – the anti-Muslim card. Swedish suburbs have over the last decade turned into fierce battlegrounds of interpretation, discredited as 'no-go-zones' in the international media and targeted by mainstream politics as hotbeds of organized crime and radicalization. The event 'Pride Järva' (a suburb of Stockholm) was, for instance, designed in the circles around the Swedish far-right party Sweden Democrats (Sverigedemokraterna, SD), and directed to march in mainly Muslim areas in order to demonstrate the Muslims' purported intolerance towards the LGBTQI+ community. Playing the 'homonationalist' card, Järva was used as a screen upon which to project conspiracist narratives of unprogressive parts of Sweden stuck in a swamp of prejudice and religious fundamentalism (Önnerfors 2018).

In front of the media, Listhaug warned against a lenient immigration policy as in neighbouring Sweden. Describing 'no-go zones', Listhaug told tales of 'parallel societies having developed in more than sixty places in Sweden'. In these no-go places, she said, were 'a large quantity of people with immigrant backgrounds'. She went on to insist that these areas festered with 'conditions of lawlessness and criminals in control'.[2]

The Norwegian minister for integration repeatedly warned against a foreign policy which she referred to as the 'Swedish condition'. The *Financial Times* wrote that the term was code for 'gang warfare, shootings, car burnings and other integration problems' in the

66   *Migration and the dangerous outsiders*

neighbouring country (Milne 2017). Listhaug's Swedish counterpart, Helene Fritzon, responded by cancelling a planned visit and dismissing the claim as 'complete nonsense'. Witnessing the rapid rise of the SD in the Swedish political landscape, mainstream political parties such as the Social Democrats or the conservative Moderaterna have increasingly turned to Norway and Denmark to find support for new (and harsher) proposals on immigration and integration. Both the Christian Democrats and Moderaterna have abandoned the 'cordon sanitaire' for the radical-right and populist SD (which for a long time had remained an exception on the European level). For the sake of the creation of a 'conservative block' ahead of the 2022 general election or any snap election before that date, both parties have subscribed to the SD's sinister narrative of the country in orchestrated terminal decline.

Although Listhaug's statements were widely debunked and dismissed as unfounded, neither she nor her party suffered at the polls. On the contrary, the FrP only rose in opinion polls in the wake of the controversy. After rewinning her seat in parliament, Listhaug continued to uphold similar rhetoric, posting on Facebook in March 2018, for example, an accusation that the Labour Party put the rights of terrorists above national security.

Forgotten people left behind

Although Finland had surely seen its fair share of wide-ranging nationalist movements, right-wing populist parties similar to those in neighbouring countries only rose to prominence in the wake of the Euro crisis in 2009, when the True Finns Party rose to prominence. Until the financial crisis, the True Finns had enjoyed only marginal support. In the wake of the crisis, their charismatic leader, Timo Soini, was quick to position his party against the EU bailout for crisis-ridden countries in southern Europe. Soini saw his party as a forceful channel for the underclass and asked, 'Why should Finland bail anyone out?'

With the EU and the European Central Bank seemingly powerless, the True Finns said that the system favoured elites over ordinary citizens. One of the party's most prominent representatives, Jussi Halla-aho, wrote on Facebook that Greece's debt problems would not be resolved without a military junta.

The True Finns were able to break up a stagnant party system, and Finnish politics came to a significant degree to revolve around them. Prior to finding success, the True Finns had been widely dismissed as merely an insignificant nuisance on the fringe of Finnish politics (Raunio 2013).

Migration and the dangerous outsiders 67

Building on the SMP's politics, the True Finns Party was highly successful in exploiting the centre/periphery divide, effectively exchanging the agrarian-focused populism of previous decades for a more general cultural divide based on a more ethno-nationalist programme. In this quest, Timo Soini adopted the phrase of the 'forgotten people', which referred to the underprivileged ordinary man neglected by the political elite.

In this formulation the political elite were presented as corrupt and arrogant, and continually accused of having suppressed the ordinary blue-collar man. Positioning themselves against the urban Helsinki-based cosmopolitan political elite (and remarkably against the Swedish minority), the True Finns Party representatives claimed to speak in the name of the 'forgotten people', mainly those working in rural areas.

Drawing on what they referred to as traditional Christian values, the True Finns Party depicted the 'forgotten people' as pure and morally superior to the privileged elite. This sort of moralist stance was widely found in the party's 2011 election manifesto, including claims of basing their politics on 'honesty', 'fairness', 'humaneness', 'equality', 'respect for work and entrepreneurship', and 'spiritual growth' (see Raunio 2013).

Like both the Danish People's Party and the Progress Party in Norway, the True Finns Party was welfare chauvinist. On ethno-nationalist grounds it emphasized first protecting native Finns but excluding others.

On this platform, a more radical and outright xenophobic faction thrived within the party. Jussi Halla-aho, who became perhaps Finland's most forceful critic of immigration and multiculturalism, led the highly conspiratorial anti-immigrant faction. Despite the insignificance of the almost non-existent Muslim community in Finland, the True Finns were still able to focus much of the country's political debate on Muslim migration. There are parallels between this rhetoric and antisemitism during the Second World War. Despite the small number of Jews in Finland, plans for their deportation to Nazi extermination camps were close to realization.

In 2012, Halla-aho was convicted of disturbing religious worship and of ethnic agitation (Dunne 2014). In 2008, he wrote the following on his blog when discussing immigration: 'Since rapes will increase in any case, the appropriate people should be raped: in other words, green-leftist dogooders and their supporters'[3] (cited in English translation on Yle Uutiset 2008). Hallo-aho described Islam as a 'totalitarian fascist ideology' and wrote that the Prophet Muhammad was a paedophile. He said that Islam, as a religion, indeed sanctified paedophilia.[4]

68 *Migration and the dangerous outsiders*

Many other examples of defiance against immigration exist amongst members of the True Finns Party. Olli Immonen, a well-known party representative, posted on Facebook in 2015 a photo of himself with members of the borderline neo-Nazi extreme-right group the Finnish Resistance Movement. Defending his actions, he wrote that he would give his life for the battle against multiculturalism. In another Facebook post, he said that he was 'dreaming of a strong, brave nation that will defeat this nightmare called multiculturalism. This ugly bubble that our enemies live in, will soon enough burst into a million little pieces'.[5]

Jussi Hallo-aho contributed extensively to the anti-immigration online forum Homma, which had been established by his faction within the True Finns Party. He continued to emphasize that these were the days that would forever mark the future of the Finnish nation. 'I have strong belief in my fellow fighters. We will fight until the end for our homeland and one true Finnish nation. The victory will be ours' (Yle Uutiset 2008).

Many other prominent populist and extreme-right associations existed in Finland, some even semi-fascist. Indeed, several parliamentarians of the True Finns Party belonged to the xenophobic organization Suomen Sisu. In the wake of the so-called refugee crisis hitting Europe in 2015, mainly from Syria, a group calling themselves Soldiers of Odin took to patrolling the street of several Finnish towns. Dressed in black jackets, decorated with Viking symbolism and the Finnish flag, they claimed to be protecting native Finns from potential violence from foreigners. It is telling that they did this despite Finland never having any Viking heritage.

In the 2015 election, with Timo Soini at its head, the True Finns Party entered government for the first time. Since then, its support diminished. After an internal split in the party, Jussi Halla-aho rose to the helm and support for the party diminished further.

Under siege

Out of the Nordic five, Iceland was the only country where fully populist parties did not thrive during most of the period examined here. Until the 2017 parliamentary election, when two at least quasi-populist parties passed the threshold and took up seats in parliament, such parties had not found significant electoral success. In that respect, we can perhaps speak of an Icelandic exception rather than a Swedish one.

However, the 2008 financial crisis, which hit Iceland especially hard, brought political upheaval and unleashed a number of populist actors.

Migration and the dangerous outsiders 69

Through the so-called Pots-and-Pans revolution that was spurred by the crisis, several protest movements emerged.

On the wave of the crisis, a completely renewed leadership took over the country's old agrarian party, the Progressive Party, which was rapidly retuned in a more populist direction: geared against foreign creditors and international institutions and, eventually, towards a degree of anti-Muslim rhetoric, which until then had been absent in the country – as there is no significant Muslim minority in Iceland.

In 2013, the young and new PP leader, Sigmundur Davíð Gunnlaugsson, came to head a coalition government with the mainstream, previously hegemonic, conservative Independence Party – which had been ousted in the Pots-and-Pans revolution.

After being exposed in the so-called Panama papers for holding a small fortune in unregistered offshore accounts, Gunnlaugsson lost leadership of the party. He responded by establishing a new one, the Centre Party, which was even more clearly nationalist populist than the PP had been while under his leadership. Gunnlaugsson was also prone to uphold a wide range of conspiracy theories. He insisted that the Hungarian-born American-based businessman George Soros had orchestrated his own demise by leaking the Panama papers. In 2019, the party was elevated by manufacturing controversy over EU energy legislation, which Iceland adopted through the EEA agreement.

Another quasi-populist party also found support in the 2017 election. The People's Party (Flokkur fólksins) was prone to uphold welfare chauvinism. In a post on Facebook in 2016, party leader Inga Sæland countered the cost of asylum seekers with helping poor Icelanders. She insisted that while poor Icelanders suffered hardship, asylum seekers, funded by the state, were living in comfort. Rhetorically, she asked whether that money might instead be better used to help poor Icelanders.

Deceit and betrayal

In 2010, the Sweden Democrats entered parliament for the first time, finally passing the threshold of relevance in Swedish politics. Until then, they had been kept firmly on the fringes of Swedish politics.

The party had been founded in 1988 out of the remains of movements closely associated with neo-Nazi forces (Bergmann 2017). Prominent early SD leaders had also been associated with neo-Nazi movements. Its first proper leader, Anders Klarström, had, for example, been involved in the Hitler-admiring Nordic National Party formed in 1956. Initially,

70 *Migration and the dangerous outsiders*

the SD, thus, had a much more extreme and xenophobic legacy than nationalist populist parties in the other Nordics.

The Sweden Democrats forcefully criticized the lenient immigration policy of the mainstream parties, insisting that it had caused segregation, rootlessness, criminality, conflict, and increased tension in society (see Hellström 2016). They described the Rosengård block complex in Malmö and other immigrant communities as ghettos that had become no-go areas for Swedes. They implied that the Social Democrats had effectively deceived and betrayed native Swedes when turning these places into foreign-held territories, occupied by Muslims who were the country's greatest foreign threat and who had even introduced sharia law on Swedish soil (Åkesson 2009b). Although never true, they still claimed that the police even hesitated to patrol these areas.

The SD's move from the far-right fringe of xenophobic and neo-Nazi extremism was first achieved after young Per Jimmie Åkesson and his cooperators took over the helm in 2005. The party was rerouted away from its previous neo-Nazi past and instead turned towards the model of the Danish People's Party, the Front National in France, and the Austrian Freedom Party (Klein, 2013).

In an ethno-pluralist 'equal but separate' doctrine, the SD avoided openly describing Swedish culture as superior. Instead, Swedish culture and identity were portrayed as being unique and firmly separated from others. Each nation was here understood to possess one ethnically determined culture. Swedish culture thus became a dividing line separating the native population from others in society, who were presented as a threat to internal social cohesion (see Hellström 2016). In the view of the SD, each nation embodied a singular culture based on ethnicity (Nordensvard and Ketola 2015). They said it was the responsibility of Swedes to protect their own culture and identity from external contamination. It was on these grounds that their 2011 manifesto stated their aim of turning Sweden back into a culturally homogeneous society, where the interests of the native population always came first.

They manoeuvred their way into a position of at least limited legitimacy, but the real tactical breakthrough came by shrewdly adopting the social democratic notion of the People's Home (*Folkhemmet*). Jimmie Åkesson claimed that the Social Democrats had abandoned their long-asserted promise of the People's Home, the all-embracing welfare society. Åkesson and his clique instead insisted that the SD was now its true representative. This was a rhetorical twist in which the SD skilfully played on the nostalgic wish to restore the national home – reverting back to a simpler and happier time in Sweden.

In staging their claim, the SD furthermore accused the Social Democrats and other mainstream parties of betrayal, of abandoning

Migration and the dangerous outsiders 71

the people and only working on behalf of their own interest or for external forces. After his death, former party leader and long-standing prime minister Olof Palme was identified as the main domestic culprit, accused by the SD of the rapid internationalization of Sweden and of promoting multicultural views.

The SD adopted the winning formula of the Danish People's Party and Geert Wilders' Freedom Party in the Netherlands. Nordic populism generally employed a narrative of linking people and culture to the nation-state, that is, in protecting the redistributive welfare state for only the ethnic population and, thus, placing migrants as a threat to it.

The new master narrative of the SD was in combining ethno-nationalism and anti-elite populism with welfare chauvinism. Jimmie Åkesson maintained that the unique Swedish welfare system could not handle too much immigration. He thus presented welfare and immigration as mutually exclusive and asked the electorate to choose between the two. This was illustrated in an SD advert in 2010: A native woman pensioner slowly moving with her wheeled walker is overtaken by a group of fast-moving Muslim women in burkas, who cash out the social security coffers before the Swedish woman arrives. The slogan read: 'Pensions or immigration – the choice is yours' (cited in Klein, 2013). In a traditional welfare chauvinistic way, Åkesson and his team thus positioned themselves as the guardians of the welfare state, claiming that voting for immigrant-friendly mainstream parties was a vote against the traditional heritage of Swedish welfare, while a vote for his party was for protecting the universal welfare system.

By stealing back the metaphor of the People's Home from the Social Democrats, the SD set out to achieve several goals at once. The first was simply to capitalize on the myth of a unifying Swedish heritage. Second, they positioned themselves as the true representatives of the welfare society, the defining factor of Swedish national identity. Third, this was simultaneously a way to criticize the current leadership of the Social Democrats for having let down the native population for a naive celebration of multiculturalism. A final positive side effect was the portrayal of the contemporary Social Democrats as deceitful and alienated elitist traitors – out of touch both with their past and present society.

While moving to the mainstream, the SD always flew their anti-immigrant flag. This was well illustrated in an open letter to the True Finns Party in 2015, written by the leadership of the SD's youth movement, warning their neighbour not to repeat Sweden's mistakes. In the letter titled 'Finland, you do not want the Swedish nightmare', they wrote that over the decades Sweden had been 'destroyed' by immigration after 'undergoing an extreme transformation from a harmonious society to a shattered one'. They said that many Swedes totally opposed

72 *Migration and the dangerous outsiders*

this system of 'mass immigration, extreme feminism, liberalism, political correctness and national self-denial' (Kallestrand et al. 2015). This mirrored Åkesson's previous positions. In a newspaper article in 2009 he framed Muslims as the greatest foreign threat to Sweden and, indeed, to Europe. In line with the Eurabia conspiracy theory he claimed that Western societies were becoming Islamized and under threat from sharia law (qtd. in Nordensvard and Ketola 2015).

Conclusion

Taken together, a clear pattern emerges across the Nordic countries, in which conspiratorial imagination and populist mobilization are intertwined phenomena occurring at all levels of political rhetoric, from party programmes to policy statements and terrorist manifestos. In various degrees among the different countries and across the populist party spectrum, the one position feeds the other. The fear of migrants and outsiders in general (including the EU as an abstract alien political actor) is utilized in order to push for the adoption of radically exclusionary politics, ranging from redesigned welfare chauvinism to outright and racist xenophobia. In the construction of all types of conspiratorial enemy images, dehumanization is a common strategy. On the one side, the dangerous 'other' is imagined as both an existential threat with almost supra-human and devastating (biopolitical) power, and on the other side an inferior being, unable to adopt to the superior culture he (deliberately) has been admitted to (by internal enemies).

To underpin such somewhat contradictory claims, the Nordic populist right-wing parties have resorted to circulating conspiracy theories such as that of 'Eurabia' and the Great Replacement. Although these conspiracy theories might not (yet) be present in official party programmes and policy statements, they still create meaning behind a populist rhetoric that attracts and most likely will attract huge proportions of Nordic electorates for the foreseeable future.

Notes

1 See 'Fremskrittspartiets handlingsprogram 2009–2013' 2009.
2 Cited in The Local 2017.
3 Police to Investigate Helsinki City Council Member's Blog 2008. Cited in English translation on Yle Uutiset, 2008.
4 Cited on mtv.fi, 2010 (Islamin yhdistäminen pedofiliaan toi Halla-aholle sakot myös hovilta 2010).
5 (qtd in English translation in Winneker 2015).

5 Conspiracy theories about the Nordic countries

Since their growth from agrarian countries to cutting-edge states with advanced industries, economies, and lifestyles, the Nordics have held a fascination for the rest of the world. Topping indices of happiness, human development, and gender equality, Finland, Denmark, Iceland, Norway, and Sweden have had a worldwide reputation for unbeatable success. However, as has been discussed in previous chapters, this image is quite recent. For instance, the myth of the Swedish model, encapsulating the idea of an exceptionally successful welfare state, only emerged in the 1930s–1960s (Ruth 1995). This myth includes the assumption that economic success also helped the Swedes eradicate such traditionally problematic phenomena as social inequality, sexual puritanism, and xenophobia (Marklund 2009: 84).

The image of Nordic prosperity is still relevant and instrumental in political arguments and campaigns. For instance, the pictures of Nordic welfare unfold in the 'I live in [a Nordic country]' meme proliferating on the Internet. It features a blonde Nordic woman who presumably narrates her life in the promised land:

> I live in Sweden. We have social security, affordable health care, strict gun laws, 5 weeks paid annual leave, and [one] year maternity leave. A stay at the hospital for one night costs about $10. Prescription drugs have an annual cap of $210.
>
> I am a school teacher in Denmark making about $61,000/year. We get free education. You don't have to pay for the doctor or the hospital, and students even get paid to learn.
>
> (Lacarpia 2015)

A teacher in Finland explains why her country's school system is the best in the world: 'We pay teachers like doctors, students enjoy

74 *Conspiracy theories about Nordic countries*

over an hour of recess, and there is no mandatory testing—the opposite of what America does'.

(Watson 2013)

The spread of the 'I live in [a Nordic country]' welfare narrative has mostly been attributed to supporters of US Democrat Bernie Sanders. His party was criticized for exploiting the image of a Nordic utopia to highlight cracks in the American welfare system, such as medical insurance, healthcare, and education (Jackson 2015). This is just one example of how mostly leftist politicians, intellectuals, and journalists utilize the image of the advanced Nordic welfare state as an exemplary standard to strive for.

It would be wrong, however, to assume that the image of the Nordics is solely positive. In the mid-1950s a number of politically conservative English-language writers critiqued Sweden by, for example, focusing on its sexual policies. They insisted that the state had too much influence over the private lives of citizens (Lennerhed 1994: 89–98). The Swedish model was challenged also from the left. In 1969, after living in Sweden for a year, the American writer and film-maker Susan Sontag criticized Swedes for being 'unbearably cold, stiff and priggish' and for avoiding conflict, even at the expense of lowering work results. Sontag also critiqued the exceptionally liberal sexual policies, such as compulsory sex education since 1955, the popularity and accessibility of pornography, as well as the ubiquity of sex shops. Sontag claimed that all these served to compensate for the Swedish lack of sensuality (Sontag 1969). Taking these claims further, in the book *The New Totalitarians*, journalist Roland Huntford argued that by establishing and encouraging liberal sexual policies, the Swedish state conspired to control its citizens by making them docile (see Lennerhed 1994: 96–97).

The real criticism of the Nordic models, however, stems from Nordic citizens' disillusionment, caused by the considerable loss of efficiency and legitimacy of the welfare systems in the last three decades (Rosenberg 2002: 180). This Nordic discontent contributed to the transformation of the Nordics' image from 'that of a well-functioning but existentially bland economic wonder into a more pluralistic, fragmented and perhaps gloomy society' (Demker, Leffler, and Sigurdson 2014: 1). When seemingly well-developed social institutions did not perform as expected, this was, as discussed in the previous chapter, often blamed on the presence of non-European migrants. With increasing globalization, conflicts related to different cultural norms have also come close to the surface in the Nordic countries. As in the case with the positive image, such negative depictions have been used strategically by politicians,

Conspiracy theories about Nordic countries 75

intellectuals, and journalists, often – although not exclusively – of the right wing.

With the worldwide rise of populism and nationalism, as well as the disenchantment with Western models of life in the post-socialist and postcolonial states, narratives about the drawbacks of the Nordic models – whether real or imagined – have appeared in a variety of genres, aiming to deliver different ideas. Narratives illuminating the supposed failure of Nordic (and Western) gender and multicultural policies emerge in conspiracy theories indicating the presence of a sinister cabal of liberal European politicians. These allegedly aim to undermine traditional family and cultural values and, by doing so, change the world in a negative way. These conspiracy theories exist in the form of Internet fake news, verbal rumours, or even stories of personal experience, and form the basis of political debates about different countries' course of development.

Despite this generic conspiratorial view, certain conspiracy theories have emerged relating to the Nordic countries' specific profiles. In the following sections conspiracy theories primarily associated with Norway, Sweden, and Denmark will be discussed. In addition, we show how other Nordic countries may play an auxiliary role by reaffirming the conspiracy narrative with additional fake news and rumours from the region.

Children and family values in the spotlight. Focus on Norway

Norway was not initially known for liberal sexual norms. The idea of a free-minded, tolerant, and sexually progressive population has been an essential part of, particularly, the Swedish welfare paradise narrative, as mentioned above. The term 'Swedish sin' emerged in the 1950s (following the 1955 *Time* magazine article 'Sin and Sweden') to refer to an open-minded Swedish attitude to sexuality. The introduction of mandatory sexual education in schools, the legalization of contraceptives, and the decriminalization of homosexuality all took place earlier than in other countries and contributed to this image. Such measures often resulted in debates on sexual policies and revealed remarkably tolerant views, which of course met criticism (Heinö 2014).

Keeping in mind the Swedish debate on sexual freedom and its worldwide reputation, it is particularly surprising that most conspiracy theories related to Nordic sexual amorality did not emerge about Sweden but instead were about Norway. Their origins may largely be due to Irina Bergseth, a Russian who moved from her native country to Norway in 2005. She married Norwegian Kurt Bergseth, and brought

76 *Conspiracy theories about Nordic countries*

along a son from a previous marriage. She also had a child with her Norwegian husband and obtained permanent Norwegian residence in 2007. In 2008, Irina filed for divorce and accused her husband of sexually abusing the children. In the ensuing court case, she lost custody of both children and had to return to Moscow. In Russia, she became a celebrity by telling intricate stories about dismal Norwegian family values on talk shows and in other media (Borenstein 2019: 163–167).

According to Irina, Norwegian bureaucrats did not acknowledge her PhD from a leading Moscow university, and instead offered her the position of a provincial schoolteacher. This is how, she says, she learned about the Norwegian school system – from the inside. Its only goal is to teach the alphabet, counting, and reading prices in the shops. Irina claims that her eldest son, previously educated in a Russian school, performed like a wunderkind compared to his Norwegian classmates. If asked by their parents to do homework, Norwegian children can make a formal complaint and the state will liberate them from their sadistic families. For this, the state employs *Barnevernet* (Norwegian Child Welfare Services), described by Irina as 'a local Gestapo' or a children's police primarily serving to save children from their birth parents.

Another striking cultural tradition Irina claims she observed in Norway was incest. According to her, this is a normal practice among Norwegians, who even lend their own children to neighbours for sexual intercourse. Irina asserts that Norway has a state plan for taking children away from birth parents and traditional families to give them away to LGBTQ couples. Norway's ultimate purpose is to make its society 100% homosexual by 2090. She claims that even now, all Norwegian leaders are from gay communities, and that removing children from traditional families corresponds to the state agenda. The public authority responsible for the protection of children in Norway is the Ministry of Childhood and Equality – according to Irina, the 'equality' in its name refers to the equality of all the forms of sexual diversity, including, for instance, paedophilia. This is promoted on all levels, she insists, claiming, for example, that the state withdrew children's fiction underlining traditional family values (*Cinderella*, Grimm's Fairy Tales, etc.) and wrote its own amoral literature instead. In Norway, the prince does not meet Cinderella but another prince.

The effect of this legal incest is, according to Irina, that many children are born with disabilities. The need to stop inbreeding is hence another reason driving the child protection services' activities. Norwegian municipalities are encouraged, but struggle, to fulfil a quota for kidnapping children from their migrant – especially Eastern European – birth parents. Irina describes how the Norwegian state offers incentives

Conspiracy theories about Nordic countries 77

with financial rewards, while ratings of the best results are published in the local newspapers. Norwegian laws facilitate the omnipotence of the Norwegian *Barnevernet*, says Irina, claiming, for example, that it is illegal for women to cry in Norway. The tears of a mother whose children are taken away by *Barnevernet* are used as proof that she is unstable or crazy, thus exacerbating her position if she tries to get them back. Irina explains that Norway considers itself the fifty-first state of the United States and follows an American agenda in promoting such laws, and also that it meddles abroad in order to introduce them. Irina concludes that Russia is the last island of the traditional family, where she can be sure about the safety of her children (Al'shaeva and Rizaieva 2013; Bergseth 2013).

As absurd as Irina's claims are, she employs clever rhetorical strategies. First, their source is authoritative and appealing. She actually lived in Norway and is able to assert that she has first-hand information. The PhD degree she claims to have, her smart appearance, and her savvy speech, all contribute to the believability of her narrative. So do her civil activities. Irina is now a head of the organization Mothers of Russia and a human rights activist fully supported by another public authority, the Children's Ombudsman of Russia. Its head, Pavel Astakhov, is known for having lobbied to ban the adoption of Russian orphans by Americans. Irina's narratives are appealing in that they connect many dots to demonstrate the sinister plot of the Norwegian (and largely Western) government to undermine traditional values. Finally, no matter how outrageous, Irina Bergseth's story resonates with the majority in Russia, because it touches on the essential topic of family and children.

Irina's narrative was on the rise in the Russian media in 2013–2014. This period coincided with the rise in Vladimir Putin's authoritarianism, with the annexation of Crimea, and with the ensuing need of the Russian state to construct propaganda narratives against the West. At this time, Bergseth's statements about Russia as the last bastion of traditional values, as opposed to 'the sodomite dictatorship' of Europe, was very timely and fit the dominant narrative that non-heterosexuals and sex-radical norms were imposed by the imperialist West to tarnish Russia (Persson 2015: 263). However, it would be too simplistic to understand Irina's narrative as merely Russian state propaganda. One should not underestimate the activity of civil society as well as the zeal of individuals in disseminating such stories. The emergence of Irina's conspiracy theory coincided with the heated debate of the 2000s on the Russian legislation project of so-called juvenile justice (*iuvenal'naia iustitsiia*). This was a set of laws the Russian government wanted to introduce to

78 *Conspiracy theories about Nordic countries*

defend children's rights in accordance with the UN Convention of the Rights of the Child. Passing these laws would have entailed taking children away from families in difficult living conditions and placing them in special institutions or with new families. Many claimed that this new legislation was imposed by the West, and there was also distrust in how the Russian state administration would implement it. This resulted in a public uproar and mobilization of a grassroots movement in defence of traditional Russian family values (Höjdestrand 2015). Irina Bergseth's narrative actually supported this public protest against the Russian state agenda and urged the state not to create a system as inhumane as the Norwegian one.

In her in-depth study of juvenile justice debates in Russia, Tova Höjdestrand concludes that not even the most skilled spin doctors of the Kremlin were capable of conjuring such a plethora of folk responses towards the new legislation (2016: 10). Similarly, Eliot Borenstein, in his recent book on conspiracy theories in Russia, notices that none of the ideological stances that have become prominent in Putin's rule can simply be ascribed to a central propaganda brain trust. Leaders typically build on what they already have to work with, that is, the fantasies which people readily provide and circulate (2019: xi). Hence, reducing the narrative of Irina and her followers to the success of Russian information warfare simplifies and narrows its complexity.

Undoubtedly, not just in Russia but also universally, people are afraid of losing their children. Earlier, this fear manifested itself in stories featuring a range of different actors with nefarious aims kidnapping children. There were stories of Jews using the blood of Christian children to bake matzo, of Roma stealing white children of aristocrats seeking rejuvenation by bathing in children's blood or of elites sexually exploiting children (Victor 1990: 61; Campion-Vincent 2006). *Barnevernet* became a new protagonist in the stories about the kidnapped children, representing the interests of the new enemies, that is to say, the LGBTQ community and politicians arguing for sexual liberation and gender equality, and complying with amoral Norwegian cultural values.

Little wonder that stories about the evil *Barnevernet* are widespread in many other countries beyond Russia. In Lithuania, Gražina Leščinskiene hit local headlines after her son was taken into care by *Barnevernet*, and, according to her, as part of the programme to fight inbreeding in Norway. Gražina's compatriot Airida Pettersen claimed that *Barnevernet* had taken her children away because her daughter was dressed too prettily, or too femininely. In Lithuania, the stories of these and other women have contributed to the belief that Norwegian authorities strive to obtain fresh, foreign children, such as Lithuanian

Conspiracy theories about Nordic countries 79

ones, to strengthen the genetic material. To counteract these beliefs, Norway's ambassador to Lithuania, Dag Halvorsen, hired a Lithuanian public relations firm, but even this did not inoculate the public against these conspiracy theories (The Local 2015b). After *Barnevernet* in 2015 had taken two children away from their Czech birth mother, Eva Michalakova, the Czech president, Milos Zeman, compared this organization to the *Lebensborn*, the institution set up by the Nazis in order to boost the Aryan race (The Local 2015a). In 2015, *Barnevernet* also took custody of all five children in a Romanian Pentecostal family. Parents Marius and Ruth Bodnariu were accused of domestic violence, which led to public upheaval in Norway and Romania (Szyma 2018: 14–15).

In another widely publicized case, Amy Jakobsen, an American citizen, testified that *Barnevernet* removed her nineteen-month-old son from her because she was still breastfeeding him (Korf 2019). An Indian couple living in Norway claimed that two of their children were taken away by child protection services because the couple fed the children with their hands, and because the infants slept in the same bed as the parents. Indian politicians interfered, and the story caused a minor diplomatic scandal (NDTV 2012). A Brazilian woman and her three-year-old daughter took refuge in their country's embassy in Oslo, after Norway's child protection services attempted to forcibly take the child into care (The Local 2013). A Norwegian citizen, Silje Garmo, requested asylum in Poland after fleeing from *Barnevernet* with her daughter (Visegrad Post 2018). This list continues with many more examples of how the representatives of many countries, including Norway itself, have turned their ire against the activities of *Barnevernet*.

While Norway remains the main protagonist in family- and children-related conspiracy theories, the examples from other Nordic countries feature by proxy, supplementing and reinforcing the anti-Norwegian narrative. For instance, the stories about malicious child protection services are very popular on the Internet forums for Russian-speaking migrants in Sweden. A migrant-to-be, for example, asks:

> Dear forum visitors, please share the information you have. How many cases when custody is taken from a Russian mother in Sweden and a child sent to the orphanage do you know? A Swede has proposed to me, but I have a child from the first marriage [...] I feel scared. Please let me know what to do.
>
> (Svenska Palmen 2012)

The interlocutors react differently: some post stories that support such doubts, others, who have lived in the Nordic countries for a long time,

80   *Conspiracy theories about Nordic countries*

respond with humour, a frequent companion of conspiracy theories (Astapova 2017: 297–299):

> Yes, children are taken away and the blood of the taken babies is added to *surströmming* [A northern Swedish speciality made of fermented herring]. The blood of the babies baptized in the Russian Orthodox Church is especially valuable. It is considered a very special delicacy served at Christmas only.
>
> (Svenska Palmen 2012)

Finland has a similar sinister reputation. Rimma Salonnen, a Russian citizen who lived in Finland, claims that after her family returned to Saint Petersburg, the Finnish child welfare services kidnapped her son Anton, and took him back to Finland in the trunk of a diplomatic car. This, she argued, was part of a secret, yet mass campaign related to the demographic crisis in Europe and the hunt for 'healthy Russian genes' (Salonen 2019). The idea that the Nordics are dying out, due to the abundance of homosexual couples, inbreeding, and the influence of the unhealthy genes of African and Middle Eastern migrants, is also reflected in a popular fake news item about Iceland. According to this story, foreign men who marry Icelandic women receive up to 5,000 US dollars, or immediately obtain Icelandic citizenship, in a public policy to prevent inbreeding. This false rumour became so popular that some Icelandic embassies abroad had to publish a rebuttal (Icelandic Review 2016). The rumours about the genetic consequences of inbreeding fortified another fake news story which asserted that Iceland used abortion to counteract the high incidence of Down's syndrome in the population (Kaspak 2017).

The Norwegian *Barnevernet* cannot respond to accusations. Client confidentiality prevents the institution from providing its version of events. As a consequence, the only source of information about these cases are desperate parents as well as irresponsible media outlets exaggerating the controversies (Szyma 2018: 3–7). But the negative image and stories about atrocities committed by *Barnevernet* also stem from real problems within the institution. Multiple media and academic publications indicate that the majority of parents (up to 55%) find interactions with *Barnevernet* distressing (Thrana and Fauske 2014: 229). Furthermore, in the case of migrants, miscommunication with *Barnevernet*, due to language difficulties, may be a problem. Finally, cultural differences related to appropriate child-rearing practices may also cause clashes (Szyma 2018: 7). For instance, as mentioned in Chapter 3, in Norway – as in the other Nordic countries – spanking is illegal and

Conspiracy theories about Nordic countries 81

criminalized, while some non-Norwegian families may find this practice normal or even essential.

The controversies around *Barnevernet* contribute to its image as an inhumane and Kafkaesque bureaucratic machine. They reflect a disillusionment with the glorified Nordic welfare state and its institutions. The complex logistical frameworks of bureaucracy offer an ideal backdrop against which conspiratorial imaginaries of organized others emerge and flourish. The whole system – consisting of *Barnevernet*, municipalities seen to compete in kidnapping children, the Ministry of Education compiling sex literature – seems to work together to achieve a specific end. As with other conspiracy theories, stories about malevolent *Barnevernet*, which supposedly aims ultimately to undermine traditional family values, stem from genuine grievances and reflect the preoccupation with the growing impact of bureaucracy and interference of the state in the life of individuals (Carey 2017: 87–96).

In conspiracy theories, the interfering party is imagined as a malign cabal plotting to achieve their own end. Recently, European right-wing politicians and activists from Poland to Estonia have claimed that they actually know who is behind the cabal. Articles, opinion pieces, and social media posts in different languages claim that Europe is governed by childless baby boomers. Since most of the high-profile European leaders do not have children of their own, these pieces claim, they have no morality or responsibility towards future generations. Their major concern is how to get elected again, not to preserve the institution of a traditional family, which is why such leaders are also favoured by sexual minorities (Kasprak 2018; Pullerits 2018).

An important part of the repertoire of such claims is the struggle against so-called gender ideologies, or 'genderism'. This is said to be imposed by foreign forces aiming to weaken nations and their traditions (Kováts 2017: 76), by the allegedly perverted activities of the LGBTQ community, by the pornographic methods of sexual education of children, and by the forcible removal of children for the purpose of their adoption by homosexual couples (Panczová 2020: TBA). 'Genderism' is synonymous with 'socialism', 'Marxism', and 'Leninism', which is used by right-wing politicians in post-socialist countries as a reminder of earlier ideological brainwashing and other socialist traumas (Apperly 2019). Or, it may spark grassroots conservative movements, such as the Eastern European parents' debates surrounding the alleged immorality in children's literature from the Nordic countries. A typical example is the debate around the translation of Louise Windfeldt's book *The Day Rikke was Rasmus/The Day Frederik was Frida* from Danish into Latvian and Lithuanian. The book caused a public uproar among Baltic

82 *Conspiracy theories about Nordic countries*

parents, who thought that the story of a boy acting as a girl for a day (or vice versa) is detrimental to children's gender identity (Kõiv 2013). Translations of the works of such authors as Ulf Stark, Moni Nilsson, and Annika Thor have caused similar debates, as these writers develop topics of corporality and sexuality, by describing, for example, teenage girls' experience of menstruation and worries about physical development (Skaf 2012). While critics of 'gender ideologies' may blame the liberal West or European Union as a whole, it seems that the Nordic countries are at the forefront of these accusations. The narratives of Nordic 'sin' and malicious child protective services – just one of its levers – are the most prominent as they are based on liberal gender policies and a struggle for gender equality. While Norway seems to attract most of the conspiracy narratives of this sort, Sweden is associated with a different conspiracy theory – that of Muslim migrants taking over the world.

Migrants to blame. The case of Sweden

In 2017, at a rally in Florida, Donald Trump used his speech to talk about migration in Europe and blamed migrants for the terror attacks in Brussels, Nice, and Paris. He added Sweden to the list saying, 'You look at what's happening last night in Sweden. Sweden! Who would believe this? Sweden...They took in large numbers. They're having problems like they never thought possible'. Nothing dramatic had happened in Sweden the previous night, and it is not clear whether Trump confused Sweden with Sehwan in Pakistan (as, indeed, riots had happened there a night before) or said this consciously in order to smear Sweden's migrant-related policies (Topping 2017).

Trump's statement exemplifies the fake news related to Sweden and other European countries as a result of their acceptance of large numbers of asylum seekers in 2015 in particular. Unlike most of the Western European countries which continue to introduce increasingly strict immigration policies, Sweden has for decades been exceptional in the field of immigration and integration. It has been easy to obtain Swedish citizenship and there has been public support of different types of migrants' associations as well as mother-tongue education. In 1996, Sweden was officially declared to be a multicultural country, and richer for that reason. However, some researchers claim that in order to uphold the idea of Sweden as a tolerant and open-minded country, the possibility that migrant minority groups might pose a challenge to the majority cultural, gender, and religious norms has often been neglected and even rejected (Demker, Leffler, and Sigurdson 2014: 9–10).

Conspiracy theories about Nordic countries 83

The debates on the issue of immigration and integration have become more heated in the twenty-first century. As discussed in Chapter 4, Sweden Democrats, a populist anti-immigration party, entered parliament in 2010 and has enjoyed a rise in popular support since 2014, having gained 17.6% in the 2018 election. Their popularity resonates with the idea that Swedish immigration and integration policies have been a national failure, and many are disillusioned with 'Swedish exceptionalism' and the principle of welfare available for all (Dahlstedt and Neergaard 2016: 124). As discussed in Chapter 2, the trope of *systemkollaps* – the total breakdown of social institutions – is used by right-wing populists to critique 'the elite'. Such disenchantment from within the country has contributed to the agenda of right-wing politicians around the world. They can, as discussed in Chapter 4, use the example of Sweden as a deterrent to highlight what happens when a Christian, 'Aryan' country takes in 'too many' Muslims and people of colour.

The whole repertoire of fake news related to migrants' crimes evolved to demonstrate how migrants' aggressive behaviour, barbaric traditions, and religious radicalism replaced local customs and led to drastic changes to society. One of these was the rumour that Sweden renamed Christmas 'Winter celebration'. This idea sprang from an innocuous headline in the Swedish daily newspaper *Sydsvenskan*, which referred to Christmas as a 'winter celebration'. Anti-Islam websites, such as *Jihad Watch* and *Voice of Europe*, noticed this headline and started pushing the notion that *Sydsvenskan* used secular terms in order to avoid offending Muslims (Evon 2018). In 2016, a number of websites published a video of people climbing on a Christmas tree in a Western-style shopping mall, claiming that it depicted Muslims attacking the holiday symbol in Sweden because it offended them (Lacarpia 2016a). Soon news outlets in other languages caught up: a Russian pro-Christian NGO published an article arguing that Christmas lights were banned in Sweden to appease Muslims (Varnava 2016). Other fake news stories stated that Swedish schools forced their pupils to pray to Allah, that refugees smashed a statue of Christ, or that the EU approved a law banning the making of white snowmen, because only racists would build them (Bergmann 2018: 159; EU vs Disinfo 2019). Other Nordic and European countries sometimes feature in such stories. Slovakian fake news about Denmark, for example, stated that the Danish government forced Copenhagen Hospitality College to take pork and wine off the menu in order not to offend Muslim students (EU vs Disinfo 2016).

Another recurrent motif is about Muslims gang-raping Swedish women, and the Swedish state concealing this. This narrative originates

84 *Conspiracy theories about Nordic countries*

from Swedish debates about several contested cases of rape by migrants, allegedly silenced by the Swedish police. For instance, in both 2014 and 2015, during the We Are Sthlm youth festival, dozens of teenage girls reported sexual harassment to the police, presumably engaged in by non-European migrants and refugees visiting the festival (Crouch 2016). The mass media outside of Sweden elaborated on this, incorporating hearsay and conjecture under alarmist headlines such as 'Raped Sweden', 'Sweden Is the Hostage of Migrants', 'The Gangs of Migrant Rapers Intimidate Sweden', 'The End of the Swedish Idyll: Migrants Kill and Rape', and 'Malmö is the European Capital of Rape' (Gashkov 2018). Fake news in different languages followed, asserting that since the arrival of non-European migrants and refugees, police in Sweden no longer investigate rape (Palma 2017). Such fake news stories also claim that, due to an increase in rape by such men, the Swedish police have introduced anti-sexual assault bracelets (Lacarpia 2016b). Another claim was that Swedish women started an online movement under the hashtag #sorry, to apologize for the depraved behaviour and clothing that lured Muslim migrants and refugees to commit sexual assault (Polygraph 2018). The 2018 Swedish law recognizing sex without consent as rape was immediately tied to the alleged multiple rapes by migrants and refugees: media outlets argued that the law had been passed because of too many rapes by these groups (Avdeev 2018). A related narrative in Finland included a visual to support the claims. There was a picture – seemingly taken somewhere in Africa – of a billboard saying 'Rape. Rape. Rape. You can do it in Finland. Refugees can do anything! Contact the Finnish embassy now' (Evon 2016a). British ultraconservatives spread another Finland-related story in which schools allegedly teach girls to have sex with immigrants. This fake news story originated from an illustration in a sexual education brochure depicting a white woman and a black man having sex (Brünnhilde 2017).

The image of women has, as previously discussed in this volume, been instrumental in anti-migrant rhetoric in many ways. Swedish women who fall in love with non-European migrants are denounced as 'fallen', a trope borrowed by Eastern European right-wing politicians from their Swedish colleagues. For instance, among many other similar posts, an Estonian right-wing Facebook group, 'Estonians against Refugee Quotas', published photos of an elderly Swedish woman with a young black man, and the condemnation of such relations.

The latter trope of Swedish women having relations with immigrant men illustrates the curious paradox of conspiracy theories. Their ideologies and elements easily contradict each other (Astapova 2020; Burstein 1959: 367). Anti-immigration conspiracy theories in and about Sweden,

Conspiracy theories about Nordic countries   85

for instance, contradict the anti-*Barnevernet* conspiracy theories which express sympathy towards migrants and their traditional values, as opposed to the corrupt values of the Nordics, and thus pity the immigrant families for their distress in a new country. However, such ideas may coexist, even in the same repertoire, especially since conspiracy theories typically blame non-European migrants for all the troubles in the Nordic countries.

Animal cruelty and bestiality. The case of Denmark

According to the conspiracy theories discussed above, Norway and Sweden are losing their traditional values, due to family policies and to immigration. Another narrative is specific to Denmark: the prevalence of devious and deliberate cruelty to animals. Compared to the previous topics, the Danish conspiracy theories related to animal cruelty are minor and less developed. However, they contribute to the overall theme of moral decay in the Nordics. As in previous cases, several real events have contributed to the image of Denmark as a country where cruelty towards animals is legalized and is a part of everyday reality.

First, the growing international movement against whaling on the Faroe Islands succeeded in drawing public attention to this traditional industry by spreading shocking pictures of dozens of slaughtered whales in a sea stained red (Berglund et al. 2018: 221). This was followed by the story of Marius the giraffe, a perfectly healthy animal killed in 2014 at the Copenhagen Zoo because he was not suitable for further breeding. Marius' body was dissected publicly in front of families with their children, and parts of the body were fed to lions. The Copenhagen Zoo followed a standard procedure of culling – removing or segregating animals from a breeding stock based on a specific trait – practised in many other zoos. But since the case of Marius became public, and since the giraffe was dissected in front of children, it received a great deal media coverage (Cohen and Fennell 2016). Fake news stories followed, claiming that Danish zoos collect people's unwanted house pets as fodder for carnivores (Viral 2017).

Contributing to this was the TED talk by an American author, Mary Roach, concerning stimulated swine orgasm at Danish pig farms, which contributed to rumours of bestiality in Denmark. Roach's talk dealt with the question of whether orgasm facilitates conception, and while there is no evidence for that in humans, Roach wanted to illustrate that this is the case with pigs. For this, Roach showed a video from Ørslevgaard farm in Denmark, where an inseminator practised the Five-Point Stimulation Plan. This is an orgasm-eliciting technique developed

86 *Conspiracy theories about Nordic countries*

by Denmark's National Committee for Pig Production, which facilitates a 6% increase in piglets. The video depicted the inseminator sitting on a sow and massaging it. This produced more discussion on the treatment of animals in Denmark, famous for its pork meat (Roach 2013).

Finally, in 2015, Denmark passed a law against bestiality, which attracted excessive attention from the international press. Even respected media outlets depicted Denmark as a barbaric country which had allowed bestiality as a legal practice until the new law. Nobody paid attention to the fact that bestiality remains legal in several European countries as well as in several US states, as many simply never bothered to introduce the same law (Holoyda et al. 2018). More misconceptions and fake news followed, claiming that bestiality and even necrophilia are accepted norms not only in Denmark but also in Sweden, or that Denmark was legalising sexual abuse of animals (Chitaladze and Tughushi 2018). The story about Danish authorities accepting the alleged opening of an animal brothel in Copenhagen, appeared in Russian, Belarusian, and Georgian news outlets, among others. The articles included an image of a dog dressed up as a street prostitute and falsely quoted Denmark's agriculture and fishery minister as saying that sex with animals is a Danish citizen's right, protected by the constitution (EU vs Disinfo 2017).

Despite being less widespread than the fake news on Norway and Sweden, the stories about bestiality in Denmark feed into the narrative about paedophilia, incest, and other sexual irregularities in the Nordics. In so doing they contribute to the grand conspiracy theory about the moral decay in these countries, orchestrated by evil politicians. Along with related stories, they serve to warn their audience against liberal policies towards 'sexual abnormalities', Muslim migrants, and similar supposed threats.

The fallen Nordics

The exoticization of remote countries often entails the idea that *they* follow very unusual traditions which are difficult for *us* to understand. In a way, the same happens to the Nordics. Their traditions and social problems, on which conspiracy theories are based, are frequently exoticized. Often, the initial information may be close to the truth, or even true, but the news outlets, and interested parties, add details or depict this information from a different angle, resulting in a distortion prone to conspiratorial interpretation. It seems that, currently, Norway has the worst reputation in Central and Eastern Europe and beyond due to the many *Barnevernet* stories and public outrage around

Conspiracy theories about Nordic countries   87

them. Sweden follows, with conspiracy theories about immigrants and refugees. Stories of bestiality in Demark are comparatively less widespread. Narratives about Finland and Iceland often complement the previously mentioned stories. Taken together, these narratives allege that the popular image of life in the Nordic countries, famous for their welfare provision, is not true. Instead, this image is deceptive, concealing the reality of the perverted and amoral Nordic lifestyle, the result of an excessive liberalism imposed by evil politicians and minorities.

The examples from this chapter challenge several potential misconceptions and existing fallacies with regard to conspiracy theories. First, it is a mistake to assume that anti-Nordic conspiracy theories, and negative representations of the Nordic countries are something new. From the 1950s, the Nordic way of life and perceived Nordic mentality have been contested abroad in a variety of ways, aiming to discourage idolization. When these stories turned into full-fledged conspiracy theories, they also borrowed motifs and elements from highly popular, and sometimes centuries-old, conspiracy theories, such as the Jewish blood libel or Satanic cults' organ theft. These stories have a strong foundation in anti-Western sentiments in the former Soviet bloc, in antisemitism in Eastern Europe, or in white supremacism in the region and beyond, among others.

This brings us to the second point: although the (mis)representation of certain countries may serve political aims and become instrumental in information warfare, one should not reduce the complexity and pragmatics of conspiracy theories to this. After the initial fascination with the term 'information warfare', scholars have shown that it has been part of political propaganda since time immemorial. In addition, the exaggeration of the centrality of 'information warfare' can lead to a one-sided understanding of the nature of misinformation (Renz 2016: 283–284). Blaming a central individual villain – like Putin – for a conspiracy theory, cannot fully reflect conspiracy theory logic either and overlooks the importance of other individuals' or groups' activities in spreading them. Too many – regardless of whether or not they support Putin – readily embellish the narratives with new fake details and spread them further, thus adding new elements to old folk stories. More than that, right-wing politicians from former Soviet countries, generally very anti-Putinist, readily draw from Putin's repertoire if it is consonant with their thoughts on migration or gender ideology. Various sources nurture conspiracy theories, including the political debates, news, and practices within the Nordic countries themselves.

Similarly, and thirdly, despite the primary role of far-right politicians in spreading anti-Nordic conspiracy theories, reducing their

88 *Conspiracy theories about Nordic countries*

proliferation to these politicians' efforts is limiting. Multiple examples from this chapter demonstrate how the idea of the 'corrupted' Nordics may be exploited in sententious preaching by religious leaders, or simply by concerned parents, regardless of their political views. Sensationalist journalism contributes a great deal to conspiracy narratives, and even respected news sources have been known to focus on stories which are themselves not that significant but which are guaranteed to get the public's attention. The most obvious example is the coverage of the Danish bestiality law, which focused on the lack of legislation and ignored the legal similarities in many other countries.

Fourth, conspiracy theories are not simply quaint and crazy stories about lizards occupying the White House. While some conspiracy theories are easy to debunk with facts, others may be based on truth, such as the dissatisfaction with *Barnevernet*'s interference with the families living in Norway. Such conspiracy theories take root because there is a kernel of truth in them: a dissatisfaction with the Nordics' state system.

Finally, conspiracy theories about the Nordic countries rarely manifest as a monolithic narrative explaining who is behind the plot, and why. Instead there are fragments, such as fake news, rumours, visuals, films, and social media posts, which contribute to the same overarching idea (even though sometimes contradicting each other). In their multiplicity and variety, however, they all serve to say that liberal Nordic values have resulted in their ultimate downfall, both moral and national.

6   Nordic noir

On 19 February 2020 the prosecutor Krister Petersson announced that the murder of Swedish Prime Minister Olof Palme in 1986, was solved. Finally. The truth, he said, would be revealed in a few months when the case went to court. The news was met with mixed reactions from experts and politicians, but it was of pivotal importance: the unsolved case was perhaps Sweden's most profound national trauma, but with the passing years and decades it had gradually slipped into history. Some say that time is the greatest healer of traumas and mysteries. There are now generations that have no personal memories of the murder, and the many new immigrants that have arrived since have little knowledge of it. Still, the unsolved case had left a lasting scar on the Swedish psyche and past emotions came rushing back with the news. But – and this is what we as scholars are trying to understand – will the promised solution to the murder satisfy the many private investigators, fuelled by conspiracy theories (see Chapter 2), who have spent decades and thousands of hours working on the case? To put it mildly, we had our doubts. Many, if not most, conspiracy theories are remarkably resilient and have a tendency to evolve. If the investigator's solution is deemed too far outside the expectations of conspiracy believers – and in the wildly divergent landscape of Palme theories, how could it not? – it is more likely that any new official revelations will only refuel the conspiracy theorists. This is what happened when, on 10 June 2020, the prosecutor declared that Stig Engström, who had died 20 years earlier, was in all likelihood the killer, although there was no hard evidence to tie him to the act (Bbc.com 2020).

In this book we have concentrated on a selection of contemporary conspiracy theories in and about the Nordic countries, but have also discussed themes prevalent in more historical ones, and traced links and continuities between them. In our material, two kinds of actors deemed dangerous conspirators frequently appear: secret elites and migrants

90 *Nordic noir*

or other outsiders. These fit the general pattern in conspiracy theory research: the sinister plot narrated in such tales typically emanates from 'above' or from the outside, or a combination of the two. In this final chapter we attempt to contextualize some of the content from earlier chapters. As we have established, there is an abundance of conspiracy theories in the Nordic countries. Several are universal, but others are more specific to the region. Some of them have been showcased to the wider world via Nordic noir storytelling in novels, movies, and TV series, which have grown in popularity over the last few decades.

Ideas and perceptions on which most of our Nordic cases rest have been imported from abroad and adapted or rephrased to local, regional, or national circumstances. In the recent decades, the Nordic countries have mostly played the role of local 'prosumers' of American conspiracy culture. Such a short historical time frame, however, tends to make us forget earlier periods, where German, French, and Russian sources also played central roles in anti-Semitic, anti-Masonic, anti-Jesuit, and other conspiracy theories with wide application. In the more recent globalized conspiracy culture, the United States has become a global centre of production and dissemination of conspiracy theories.

The Nordic countries increasingly turned towards English as a second language after the Second World War. Language proficiency is an important element in the global flow of cultural products. It is small wonder that American conspiracy culture came to dominate, due to the country's dominance in global politics, economics, and popular culture. Finland, delicately balanced politically between East and West during the Cold War period, is a special case. It seems that the country was one of the routes whereby an earlier, intermittently active line to Russia continued. Others included the long-standing route taken by Soviet conspiracist propaganda from the Stalin era through European communist parties, including in the Nordic countries. Earlier, Russian refugees fleeing the revolution were vital in promoting the *Protocols of the Elders of Zion*. In later periods, Finland was one of the routes whereby, as part of the disinformation campaign dubbed 'Operation Infektion', conspiracy theories about HIV/AIDS spread to Western countries from Russia (Qiu 2017).

While many of the exogenous conspiracy theories circulated and played some role in shaping the narrative of conspiracy tales in the Nordic countries, they had to be adapted to local circumstances, fears, and interests in order to take hold as something more than mere oddities. The home-grown theories may have adopted deep structures from outside sources, but they were addressing local themes from the start.

Local events and global flows

In the contemporary period, the best-known Nordic conspiracy theories involving ideas of secret elites have sprung from traumatic national events that have triggered social insecurities. In addition to the murder of Olof Palme, some of the prominent examples have included, as noted in earlier chapters, the sinking of the MS *Estonia*, the terrorist attack at Utøya, and the 2008 financial crisis in Iceland. The latter revolves around larger economic questions, and while the financial crisis in Iceland was related to global issues, and thus was part of a much larger set of conspiracist interpretations of large-scale events, the economy is and has been a recurring topic. Some of these have been very local or regional, expressing and/or enlarging local conflicts. In Norway, for instance, there are a host of conspiracy speculations relating to the placement of the main Oslo airport. This was, over several decades, a highly contentious issue since it was related to important economic benefits.

Similarly, there are still important conspiracy rumours and theories relating to the rural–urban divide covered in Chapter 3, in the shape of the origin of the wolf packs in Sweden and Norway. The different regional policies of Sweden and Norway, where the latter has tried to halt depopulation of rural, agrarian areas to a much greater degree, may have influenced the level of reactions to wolves. In both countries, mainstream media and public discourse are largely positive towards larger populations of wild carnivores. But there is a subcurrent of hostility echoing older folklore with its fear of wolves and linking to more recent conspiracy theories. A small subset of landowners and hunters within some organizations have been active in promoting the claim that wolves have been intentionally introduced by some despicable actor.

In Norway, conspiracy theories that environmentalists or other 'elite' groups have 'farmed' wolves and placed them in the wild have thrived to such a degree that the genetic origin of wolves was recently investigated on the order of parliament. Norwegian smallholders have classically been sheep farmers, and some see wolves as the final straw in a whole range of threats to their subsistence and livelihood (Nijhuis 2019). Their concerns are voiced through regional political representation, an important aspect of Norwegian democratic institutions. In addition, decentralized, rural-oriented demographic politics have been important, favouring a medium-sized agrarian party that carries these concerns onto the national stage. Children's safety has been amongst the main concerns regarding tales of wolves roaming around human habitation, as well as attacks on livestock and pets.

92 *Nordic noir*

This has also been a topic of Finnish controversy, but – perhaps due to its proximity to Russia – it seems to have gone mostly free of the conspiracist speculation about origins. It seems that compared to Norway, Swedish conspiracy theories about the wolf population have been more marginal and more often point to the state. Another recurring narrative in Sweden is that wildlife parks release wolves into the wild when their population becomes too high. Climate change conspiracy theories show similar, but not identical, connections to particular economic and cultural allegiances.

Other well-known, if not widely upheld conspiracy theories in the Nordics spring from exogenous impacts on a more global scale. Conspiracy theories concerned with 9/11 are the most prominent example. They set a tone in place and facilitated the creation of a, predominantly online, Nordic subculture that looked to international conspiracy cultural 'alternative media' and their interpretations of ongoing events for cues. Global events were then interpreted within conspiracist frames. The financial crisis of 2008–2009 was one such international event. How the political establishment handled the situation influenced reactions. What was widely interpreted as a lack of accountability by the 'banksters' angered many people and fed into established conspiracy narratives of several kinds. In the Nordic version, the main villains were generally portrayed as the worldwide 'bankster' conspiracy of plutocrats, Jews, and/or Illuminati.

Iceland was hit especially hard in the financial crisis of 2008, leading to the fostering of several conspiracy theories. Amongst those upholding several such tales was Sigmundur Davíð Gunnlaugsson, who became the country's prime minister in 2013. After being exposed by Wikileaks in the so-called Panama Papers for his family's small fortune held in unregistered offshore accounts, Gunnlaugsson was ousted as prime minister and later also lost leadership of his party. He responded by constructing his own party, the Centre Party, which was a more clearly nativist populist forum than the Progress Party, which he had exited. Gunnlaugsson, for instance, insisted that George Soros, through the leaking of the Panama Papers, had orchestrated Gunnlaugsson's demise as prime minister. In the 2017 general election, the Centre Party won more than a tenth of the vote. It was then elevated further in 2019 by manufacturing controversy around the EU energy legislation, which Iceland adopts through the European Economic Area agreement.

Viral fears: conspiracy and the body

Health and disease are of central importance in many Nordic conspiracy theories. The general environment following 9/11 enabled the growth of

Nordic noir 93

anti-vaccine campaigns and related conspiracy theories. The swine flu epidemic of 2009 and the corresponding anti-vaccine activities had, however, a slightly different background. They drew on established conspiracy theories about vaccines from several quarters. The MMR scare from the late 1990s to the early 2000s, when the triple vaccine against measles, mumps, and rubella was erroneously said to cause autism, was only one of the sources. Others were related to alternative theories of illnesses and cures circulating among a panoply of subcultures. Alternative therapies such as naturopathy and homeopathy constituted an international network of interested parties, and both practitioners and patient groups played a part as local prosumers, in adapting and disseminating conspiracy theories.

In this instance, the sources for Nordic conspiracy theories were much broader. While English was the lingua franca, stories from, for example, Austria, the Netherlands, and Russia were seamlessly integrated into Nordic discussions. Vaccines contained 'nano-chips' that could control your mind, kill you, or merely make sure *They* knew where you were at all times. Whatever vaccines were seen to 'actually' do in this discourse, one thing was clear: they rarely worked to protect against illness, but they rather fed money into the pockets of 'Big Pharma' and other allies of the global conspiracy. And it is almost solely in the categories of 'allies of the conspiracy' we find the conspiracist representations of Nordic actors, as local authorities and personal enemies were given the role of representatives of *Them*. Nevertheless, the anchoring of conspiracism in established subcultures, deeper world views, and in relating to family health concerns determined that this aspect of conspiracy culture continued through to the 2020 Coronavirus outbreak.

Some of the specific outlets lost influence or were discontinued, but those that continued, like the websites *Nyhetsspeilet* (The News Mirror) in Norway and *Vaken* (Awake) in Sweden, stuck to their guns, and many of their activists continued their battles during the new pandemic. Reception of COVID-19 conspiracy theories varied over time, running the international gamut from being 'fake news' – sometimes to sell the vaccine that *would* kill us – to being an international bioweapon made by whomever the current narrator wanted to blame. These could be the Chinese authorities, the CIA in the United States, or that perennial scapegoat 'the Zionists'. Bill Gates – through his charitable foundation – in conjunction with Big Pharma was another culprit.

As predicted by Barkun's (2003) concept of stigmatized knowledge claims, conspiracy believers from different ideological backgrounds had discovered anti-vaccine conspiracy theories and put them to use. As they did so, there was a partial fusion between religious and political horizons, with the relevant parts of the far left, far right, conservative Christians, and 'New Age' believers finding common ground.

94　*Nordic noir*

All of this points to an integrated, international development where Nordics and other 'critics of globalism' come together in anti-globalization conspiracy theories. It also points to an important element in how local and ideologically varied adaptations are made easier. As conspiracy theories circulate, they follow a style of narration where the framework of an evil conspiracy behind current events serves as a ready-made theory, available for immediate use. It can be filled by whichever event is ongoing, and whatever the concerns of the group or entrepreneur. As we know, conspiracism means that concerns are often combined, which explains the following diatribe from a participant in a Norwegian anti-child protection services group when schools were closed as a protective measure against the spread of COVID-19:

> This is very important. The schools are closed so that 5G may be installed in secret. The goal is to install 5G in all schools before mid-April, to kill the children. When they show signs of radiation damage (which they will then call 'Corona virus'), they will force the children to take lethal vaccines, which contain the virus, so that they die from BOTH radiation and the virus – which they'll only get from the vaccine.[1]

While the tone in the post above is more prophetically apocalyptic than most, it points to several ongoing concerns and how they were employed during the early phase of the handling of COVID-19. The new threat was fitted into narratives that already existed. For many, the real threat was the government, in tune with older, US-inspired narratives. For others, as in the quote above, the threat was vaccines, the new 5G technology, or both. All could be combined. They also combined successfully with the fear of external enemies, working, where possible, with the enemy within.

Counter-subversion

As we have seen, this narrative – a type of counter-subversion mythology – has been in place in the Nordic countries since at least the eighteenth century. Jesuits were a popular early contender in the Protestant Nordics. However, the most commonly proposed agents of such conspiracy theories were the Freemasons and the Jews, in the Nordic as well as in many other European countries. Jews were accused of forming – or aspiring to form – a state within a state. As discussed in Chapter 4, the entry of Jews into Denmark and Sweden was severely restricted or, as in Norway, barred altogether between 1814 and 1851. Following the Second World War, the Nordic countries, and especially Sweden, were

Nordic noir 95

until the mid-1970s open to labour immigration. From then on, it has instead been refugees who have increased their presence in the region. As they have in large part been from the Middle East and North Africa, this has contributed to fuelling conspiracy theories about Muslims. In the post–Second World War period representatives of nativist populist political groups and parties, as well as sections of the general public, continually displayed negative attitudes against foreigners, deemed culturally distant. But it is only in the last decades that these views have spread and been articulated as distinctly conspiracist, with Muslims accused of plotting to take over Europe, including the Nordics. As in earlier centuries, dangerous outsiders are often claimed to be helped by, or in alliance with, native elites. Such allegations, as discussed in Chapter 5, are also common in conspiracy theories about the Nordics spread on the Internet in Russia, the Baltic countries, and Central Europe. In these narratives the ordinary citizens in the Nordic countries, and especially in Sweden, are depicted as naive and the political elite as intentionally harming society.

This pattern has also been visible in certain varieties of subversion myths regarding gender and family. Gender, sexuality, and family arrangements connect – or even underpin – many conspiracy theories about plotting elites and dangerous outsiders. In both historical and contemporary cases, we have seen that young women, or even children, are depicted as victims of a conspiracy. Common tropes in transhistorical and transcultural narratives present kidnapping, rape, and murder as crimes committed via witchcraft and by Satanic cults involving conspiring elites or dangerous outsiders.

In other conspiracy narratives, women are not victims. One unusual example here is Greta Thunberg, whose highly public zealousness in the fight over climate change politics has made her the target of intense and hate-filled attacks. This includes numerous conspiracy theories accusing her of being a fanatic tool of *Them*, with a variety of actors, such as, for example, George Soros or Bill Gates, being the real forces behind her. She has also been made a topic of Americanized culture wars by being presented as 'antifa' – in right-wing conspiracist lingo not merely a radical left 'anti-fascist' but a far-left terrorist – and her image has been manipulated to appear with ISIS terrorists.

The conspiracy theories about Thunberg as a tool of evil others, and the denigrating language in which they are framed, are characteristic of many of the conspiracy theories concerned with family, gender, and sexuality. Those propagating them are not only feeling culturally threatened and thus demanding adherence to conservative gender roles. They are also calling for stricter social hierarchy in terms of gender and

96 *Nordic noir*

age: (other) people should know their true place in society. They should accept their position as inferior in worth and status. Greta Thunberg does not conform to this hierarchical thinking. She is a mere teenager, engaging in global political issues and getting recognition and a large following because of this. She thus, according to those who take a dislike to her, has occupied a higher status than she should. This perceived violation of social norms is accentuated by her being female – 'a mere girl'. Her denigrators also stress her Asperger's diagnosis. As young, female, and 'on the spectrum' (of autism), she is triply disqualified, and her denigrators use the combination of all three elements to refuse her the status of having her own agency.

These general attitudes are present in many anti-feminist conspiracy theories, in which women are criticized for claiming agency and power, such as sexual power. This is strongly expressed in the online Incel ('involuntary celibates') subculture, which also attracts participants from the Nordic countries. While most of the Incel subculture may be inclined towards self-help, some voices are actively male (and white) supremacists arguing for a forced redistribution of females. Other versions of this discursive focus on female sexuality can be found in a more politically familiar form on the far right. In those circles, as discussed in Chapter 3, women are, for example, blamed for consorting and sleeping with non-Nordic and non-Christian men. In both of these examples, misogyny is quite apparent.

These topics also call, as we have seen, on deeper issues relating to the historical organization of society. Concerns over choice of sexual partners, and that women behave in ways that reflect badly on the patriarchal family, thus threatening the status of the husband/father are, as discussed, ubiquitous throughout history. In conspiracy narratives from the late nineteenth century onwards, this was articulated mostly as fear of the lecherous 'oriental' in the shape of, for example, 'the Jew'. With the lessening of the power of the patriarchy through policies of gender equality, and especially with the rise of feminism, the narrative partially changed. Then, through their choices, women could instead be both victims and agents of subversion. Within the milieu of Nordic nativist populists, conspiracy theories relating to family, gender, and sexuality present concerns about the purity of the Nordic race, and the dangers of racial mixing. In that way, women may be considered to subvert what is perceived as natural family and gender relations and hence, have to be controlled and policed. The most extreme instance of such conspiracist thinking is that of the Norwegian terrorist Anders Behring Breivik, discussed in several chapters in this volume. Wrath and conspiracy theories directed against women breaking dominant gender norms is not new. But it seems that they

Nordic noir 97

are currently spread wider than before and, in a somewhat toned-down fashion, are finding a place in even mainstream public debate.

Patrolling the borders: the enemy outside

Conspiracy narratives involving gender, elites, and outsiders are rarely consistent or coherent. Male enemies might simultaneously be weak and strong, cunning and stupid, and Nordic women might be both targets and agents of conspiracies. And it is not only the 'acceptable' forms of femininity that are contested through conspiracy theories. Masculinity has been, and continues to be a central topic, albeit often seen through the frame of women and children as threatened victims. However, images of masculinity are often themselves contradictory and conflicting: Jewish men, for example, are often depicted as deeply alien and cosmopolitan, hence dangerous, yet simultaneously effeminate and weak. Muslim men are seen to embody medieval and misogynist values, aiming to enslave Nordic women and undermine the good Nordic family. Class, too, comes into play: conspiracy theories focusing on elite men seducing poor working-class boys were at one time part of left-wing rhetoric, as discussed.

Homosexuality – mostly male, but also female to a lesser extent – is, as shown in Chapter 5, a strong theme in conspiracy theories about the Nordics. These narratives construct an upside-down world, where the least fertile regions of Europe accuse the most fertile Europeans of stealing their children to make up for a lack of their own. This imagined lack of fertility among the Nordics is claimed to be caused by 'homonormativity', which again is considered an attack on both 'natural' sexuality and on the traditional (nuclear) family, whose children are said to be stolen and redistributed by the state. These final elements are central to the narrative of child protection services being part of a large conspiracy. These narratives partially address real concerns regarding the role of the state versus families concerning the parents' rights over children and their correct upbringing. But mostly these narratives serve to enforce the definition of 'naturalness' regarding earlier norms of gender and sexuality. In such conspiracy theories the Nordics are depicted as wealthy outsiders who challenge these norms, thus breaking 'the natural order', which is upheld and defended by 'the good authorities' of, for example, Russia. These good authorities thus protect their people against the rot of foreign influence and stop it from leaking inside their own nation.

Patrolling the borders of femininity and masculinity works both ways. Ideas of femininity implicate ideas of masculinity and the other way

98 *Nordic noir*

around. In the case of the extreme right as represented by Breivik, for example, we see how his hatred of particular groups of women underlines his perverted fictional male ideal: the blonde Nordic crusader against detrimental 'cultural Marxists' inside, and dangerous Muslims on the outside. In both cases, gender as a concept and analytical category becomes irrelevant; in the first case because ideology transcends the boundaries of gender roles; in the second because the perceived fecundity of the foreign female is a part of the threat. In the end, they all partake in a nature foreign to 'the Nordic' and are part of the same threat.

The extreme and far right are particularly focused on threats from outside and on closing borders to combat alien menace. Early on, this was internationally mirrored in how the COVID-19 coronavirus was represented as a foreign bioweapon (DeCook 2020). The other option, focused on the enemy within, presented the threat of the virus as exaggerated, or even invented, by political rivals. At the time of writing, the same conspiracy theories were present in the Nordic countries. They had not however, gained substantial traction, but circulated mainly among committed conspiracists. The extreme right was reported to be more interested in the revolutionary possibilities presented by a society in disorder (Expressen, 23 March 2020).

Nordic noir: conspiracy narratives as detective fiction

It is not surprising that there are many conspiracy theories focusing on sexuality, gender, and the family. Like questions of health and the body – disease, treatments, vaccinations – these topics speak to the very heart of society. They are at the intersection of public policies and the intimate and private lives of citizens, interacting with the topic of state and power as cultural narratives, like fiction. A similar dynamic is also seen in one of the more popular forms of fiction, the detective novel, where so-called Nordic noir literature not only depicts Nordic family and gender roles, but also uses threats against them explicitly in the construction of the plot. The 'genre' is also driven by a tradition of incorporating explicit political critique into the narrative. Local flavour is evoked through the close description of landscapes and the narrative tension between capital and the welfare state. Many of the most celebrated novels of the 'genre' are neither particularly 'noir' nor specifically Nordic in their origins: the Nordic contributions consist of a 'diverse collection of authors and novels from five different countries and numerous crime fiction sub-genres' (Bergman 2014). They are linked together as exemplars of a 'genre' mostly from outside the Nordic countries, by (misleading) ascriptions of extreme violence, sexualization, and

Nordic noir 99

liberal gender roles, but also by the focus on the Nordic landscape as a psychological mirror of both heroes and society. As imagined on the covers, the landscape is bleak, cold, and hostile. This view of Nordic nature can be as much a part of the 'exotic' appeal as the organization of society, and both serve to set the scene for the inevitably hidden social evil the reader is about to discover. Topics of family, sex, and gender, in combination with those of state and hidden forces within an almost 'Orientalist' frame (cf. Stougaard-Nielsen 2016), are thus addressed both within detective fiction and conspiracy theories.

This is no coincidence. As Luc Boltanski (2014) notes, detective novels share with conspiracy theories the strategy of calling into question the reality of what is presented as real, more specifically the 'official narrative' about reality. They rely however, on the stabilizing force of 'institutions dependent on the state, so that the *mystery* can stand out against this background' (Boltanski 2014: 25). When institutions, state, and procedures are local, the mystery must stand out against, and cast doubt on, local realities. Detective fiction thus inevitably concerns the state of the body politic, and invariably the condition and moral status of those representing the state. In this way, they partially overlap with spy novels. The detective novel is concerned more with the strictly internal and local, whereas the spy novel confronts the logic of territory with that of flows: 'forces that flow throughout the territory and put it at risk'. This is a logic that echoes and is related to earlier, far-right crime novels and conspiracy theories. There is an older school of Nordic crime novels with a history of presenting contemporary political analyses that included conspiracy theories, such as the intensely racist, antilabour, and antisemitic fiction of Øvre Richter Frich (1872–1945). The clues uncovered by the hero in this version point towards both internal subversion and dangerous outsiders. They express and mirror far-right anti-Semitism of its time, and they point towards the fear of dangerous outsiders of today.

The critique of the state in contemporary Nordic detective fiction may seem to mirror the right-wing, anti-state ethos seen in the American traditions they borrow from. That is, however, misleading. The critique of the state in emblematic Nordic noir comes from the (far) left, and concerns promises unfilled. A central theme is the dark side of the welfare state. This is noticeable in what is now considered the origins of Nordic noir: Maj Sjöwall's and Per Wahlöö's ten-volume police-procedural series *Novel of a Crime,* published between 1965 and 1975. One theme is the way in which the welfare state has failed those who most need it, often with a focus on families and children. A recurring topic is the tension between the ideals of the welfare state and how they

100 *Nordic noir*

in reality are corrupted by the (narrative) realities of capitalism, neo-liberalism, and manipulation by wealthy, semi-secret elites (cf. Robbins 2017). Against some external, anti-statist readings of the critique of the welfare state, the problem unfolding is due to the confluence of business interests and the powers of the state. Capital and the state are, if not a two-headed monster, a partnership that creates and upholds the problems revealed by the hero or heroine.

Often police officers, the female heroines of these murder mysteries, give state power a female face, while at the same time exposing the troubling parts of institutional and broader social conditions. Again, mirroring conspiracy culture, the safety of the family and the purity of the state are under threat. Detectives and their family are potential victims, children are prominent victims, and institutions are corrupted by both internal and external forces. In Nordic conspiracy culture there is, still, often a presumption of a generally functioning state; in detective fictions like police procedural murder mysteries, it is a necessary condition. Without a functioning order being policed, there could be no murder mystery, only murder (cf. Robbins 2017: 55). In conspiracy culture we note that, paradoxically, an assumption of a functioning state is prevalent even among Nordic sovereign citizens, whose ideology presents the state as evil and its regulatory powers as utterly illegitimate. They may claim freedom from legal constraints, yet appeal to state institutions to redress grievances against the same state (cf. Dyrendal 2017). In the police procedurals of Nordic noir, there is often a stress on even the excessive following of rules, preventing the hero from seeking revenge. As a true agent of the state, the detective should stay within the bounds of the rules. In the same vein, conspiracy believers often call on the state to follow the 'right procedures'. In both, there is a call for a disinterested, neutral 'procedural justice' (cf. van Prooijen 2019) for the state to function correctly and to redress what is wrong.

The political critique of the state from the political left thus takes on many of the same issues as conspiracy culture: the failure of the welfare state to care for children and to protect against abuse by both relatives and larger organized forces. It is typically the latter that are engaged in the mystery and conspiracy. The heroine and her family are in danger in detective fiction as they are in conspiracy narratives about child protection services both inside and outside the Nordics. Both types of narratives of the Nordics share tropes regarding the state, evil elites, the family, sex, and gender. The state and secret elites may act together, but there still remains the possibility to call on the former against the latter.

While the narratives of Nordic noir and conspiracy culture thus mirror and address common topics and grievances, they does so only partially.

Nordic noir 101

The concerns over global flows, the threats to the state from outside forces, and the almost total corruption of the state by subversive actors that we also see in conspiracy narratives, are all but absent from crime novels. This is, of course, not surprising: the murder mystery in the police procedurals that dominates the novels of Nordic noir nearly precludes this broader perspective. The common ground of Nordic conspiracy theorizing and Nordic noir is found in their mixing of the local contexts and the comforting allure of the known. When the topics, the tropes, and the villains are given local faces – as also happens with global conspiracy narratives – they match, but in the important conspiracy narratives addressing global flows, dangerous 'globalism', or 'great replacements' they diverge.

Nordic exceptionalism?

The conspiracy narratives flowing globally via social media are central to Nordic conspiracy narration as well. In this sense, there is no Nordic exceptionalism. The contents, as noted above, have to strike a local chord, and in so doing, we have seen that the tropes and concerns of the conspiracy theories of one period often become similar to those of earlier episodes. This seems frequently not to be because of an established cultural narrative being traduced, but because of repetition of topics and concerns, such as abuse of power or threat to health, family, or nation. In the imaginary of villainy, conspiracy theories are melodrama, and, in maximizing the evil nature of conspiracy, the atrocity tales will become similar: the victims are as blameless as possible and the crime as horrible as necessary to mobilize emotion and, more theoretically, collective action.

In the Nordic states as elsewhere, conspiracy theories express conflict and relate to distrust. Some are the result of feelings of displacement and threats to cultural norms, activated by, for example, increased migration. Multiple political actors both inside and outside the Nordic nations stand ready to use such emotions and employ conspiracy theories as crisis narratives to strengthen distrust and partisan division. Conspiracy theories about the role of the state in family relations, about gender, immigration – and, to some extent, climate change – express such political divisions. While interpersonal trust continues to be high, and institutional authorities mostly continue to hold respect, these are among the most successful conspiracy theories. However, if we look at it in the longer term, relationships between rulers and ruled, experts and non-experts, have changed. Rising populist political forces distinguish between 'the elites' and 'the people', with representatives of the people being purer and more reliable. Equally, knowledge has become

102 *Nordic noir*

'democratized', or, rather, become the property of consumer rights: if consumers do not like the product, they have a right to something they like better. Official statistics about immigrant crime or climate change are successful examples of this.

Usually, profound conspiracy narratives have, however, not been very successful in the Nordics. They tend to reach few and gain fewer adherents. They rarely influence practical politics. Some have thrived for a time, when they addressed topics that were relevant, at the time emotions ran high and uncertainty reigned, but afterwards they have drifted back into the margins, where lack of visibility tends to kill them off. As noted by Uscinski and Parent (2014) when studying the United States, most media coverage of conspiracy theories in the Nordic countries is negative, sometimes harshly so. But conspiracy theories both individually and as a family of narratives have certainly become much more visible, due to the Internet and social media. While other forms of theodicy have receded, conspiracy theories have become more readily available as a possible cultural narrative to explain evils around in society. They are partially available as a result of a tradition of American conspiracy narratives, both as entertainment and as political discourse. As such, they do not so much push out competitors like, for example, apocalypse prophecies, as they are adapted into them. Conspiracy narratives are integrated into subcultures, both religious and political, alternative and mainstream, serving to shape global discourse into local relevance.

In the Nordic countries, again as elsewhere, these nodes of conspiracy culture thus serve as 'conspiracy brokers' (Leal 2020). This is a vital role in the circulation of conspiracy theories: the brokers adapt narratives so that others, critics included, become more likely to amplify them. As long as the adapted narratives appeal to partisan identities and/or arouse strong emotion, social media logic and ease of response increase the chances of amplification, keeping the conspiracy narratives in circulation. Brokers are not originators; they are not the 'real' entrepreneurs, but they are vital because they are situated to spread conspiracy theories to new networks of potential believers. The role of conspiracy brokers also becomes central when conspiracy narratives are disseminated in sociopolitical top-down processes. This book has centred mostly on theories spreading from the 'bottom up' or from special (political) interest groups. Currently, the main source of conspiracy narratives seems increasingly to be related to such conspiracy brokers disseminating what originates from the outside as political strategies in active mis- and disinformation.

Nordic noir 103

In conclusion, the Nordic countries are not particularly exceptional when it comes to the spread and impact of conspiracy theories, but they still have their own regional nuance. The contextual meaning of conspiracy theories in the Nordic countries is often distinct from that of other countries, because – as we have illustrated in these pages – cultural and historical developments and idiosyncrasies are very important. They help shape our understanding of the world we live in, our hopes and dreams, and the conspiracy theories we choose to believe – or not. And while those same conspiracy theories do not repeat themselves in exactly the same way throughout history, they frequently rhyme, as we mentioned in Chapter 3. Plots, perpetrators, and particularities reflect historically contingent circumstances, but the underlying dynamics remain the same – also in the Nordic countries.

Note

1 Our own translation. In order to preserve anonymity, we will not here disclose which of the myriad of open or semi-open anti-CPS groups this is from.

Bibliography

Aase, R. K. (2009). *Frimurernes hemmeligheter. Fortalt fra innsiden*, Oslo: Kagge.

Aftonbladet. (1992). Jag tvingades fly för livet. Forskare nära att bli offer för satanisterna. *Aftonbladet*, 25 November, p. 6.

Aftonbladet. (1993). Polisen gräver efter 25 barnlik i Sockholmsförort. *Aftonbladet*, 9 February, p. 1.

Ahlander, J., Vaish, E., and O'Donnel, J. (2019). Nordic Trust Tarnished by Money Laundering Scandal. [online] *Reuters*. Available at: www.reuters.com/article/us-europe-moneylaundering-nordics-trust/nordic-trust-tarnished-by-money-laundering-scandal-idUSKCN1RF1EN [Last visited 14 January 2020].

Ahtokari, R. (2000). *Salat ja valat: vapaamuurarit suomalaisessa yhteiskunnassa ja julkisuudessa 1756–1996*. Helsinki: Suomalaisen Kirjallisuuden Seura.

Al'shaeva, N., and Rizaieva, N. (2013). "[How Norway Lives]." Livejournal. 2013. https://eto-fake.livejournal.com/1179734.html. [Last visited 10 October 2020].

Andersson, L. (2018). Lena Andersson: 'DN har byggt en kult kring de 18 sextrakasserade kvinnorna.' [online]. Available at: www.tv4.se/klipp/va/3969252/lena-andersson-dn-har-byggt-en-kult-kring-de-18-sextrakasserade-kvinnorna [Last visited 13 November 2020].

Andersson, L. M. (2000). *En jude är en jude är en jude…Representationer av "juden" i svensk skämtpress omkring 1900–1930*. Lund: Nordic Academic Press.

Ankarloo, B. (1987). Sverige: det stora oväsendet 1668–1676, in B. Ankarloo and G. Henningsen (eds.). *Häxornas Europa 1400–1700. Historiska och antropologiska studier*. Stockholm: Institutet för rättshistorisk forskning, pp. 248–275.

Apperly, E. (2019). "Why Europe's Far Right Is Targeting Gender Studies." *The Atlantic*. June 2019.

Arter, D. (2010). The Breakthrough of Another West European Populist Radical Right Party? The Case of the True Finns. *Government and Opposition*, 45(4), 484–504.

Astapova, A. (2017). "In Search for Truth: Surveillance Rumors and Vernacular Panopticon in Belarus." *Journal of American Folklore*, 130(517), 276–304.

106 *Bibliography*

Astapova, A. (2020). Rumours, Urban Legends, and the Verbal Transmission of Conspiracy Theories, in M. Butter and P.Knight (eds.). *Routledge Handbook of Conspiracy Theories*. London: Routledge, pp. 391–400.

Avdeev. (2018). "V Shvetsii Vstupil Zakon Ob Obiazatelnom Nedvusmyslennom Soglasii Na Seks [In Sweden, a Law about the Compulsory Sex Consent Was Introduced]." *TJournal*. https://tjournal.ru/flood/73049-v-shvecii-vstupil-v-silu-zakon-ob-obyazatelnom-nedvusmyslennom-soglasii-na-seks [Last visited 10 October 2020].

Barkun, M. (2003). *A Culture of Conspiracy*. Berkeley: University of California Press.

Bartholdy, N. G. (2009). Det Antimasonianske Societet – antifrimureri eller pietistisk loge? *Acta Masonica Scandinavica*, 12, 9–39.

Bartlett, J., and Miller, C. (2010). *The Power of Unreason. Conspiracy Theories, Extremism, and Counter-Terrorism*. London: Demos.

Bawer, B. (2012). *The New Quislings: How the International Left Used the Oslo Massacre to Silence Debate about Islam*. Broadside e-books.

Bbc.com. (2018). *Olof Palme Murder: Swedish Police Examine 'New Lead' in Unsolved Case*. [online]. Available at: www.bbc.com/news/world-europe-44225024 [Last visited 14 January 2020].

Bbc.com. (2020). *Olof Palme murder: Sweden Believes It Knows Who Killed PM in 1986*. [online]. Available at: www.bbc.com/news/world-europe-52991406 [Last visited 12 October 2020].

Bellamondo. (2011). *9/11: The Sensible Doubt* [22 min. documentary] [video]. Available at: www.youtube.com/watch?v=Qq3wPOvhjp8.

Berggren, L. (1999). *Nationell upplysning. Drag i den svenska antisemitismens idéhistoria*. Stockholm: Carlsson Bokförlag.

Berglund, J., Boström, J., Clausen, P., Gamfeldt, L., Gundersen, H., Hancke, K., Hansen, J. L. S. (2018). *Biodiversity and Ecosystem Services in Nordic Coastal Ecosystems: An IPBES-like Assessment. Volume 2. The Geographical Case Studies*. Copenhagen: Nordisk Ministerråd.

Bergman, K. (2014). The Captivating Chill. Why Readers Desire Nordic Noir. *Scandinavian-Canadian Studies*, 22, 80–89. https://scancan.net/bergman_1_22.htm [Last visited 27 March 2020].

Bergmann, E. (2017). *Nordic Nationalism and Right-Wing Populist Politics: Imperial Relationships and National Sentiments*. London and New York: Palgrave Macmillan.

Bergmann, E. (2018). *Conspiracy & Populism: The Politics of Misinformation*. London: Palgrave Macmillan.

Bergmann, E. (2020). *Neo-Nationalism: The Rise of Nativist Populism*. London: Palgrave Macmillan.

Bergseth, I. (2013). *[Marsh to Protect Children]*. www.irinabergset.ru/blog/документальный-фильм-марш-в-защиту-детей-с-ириной-бергсет [Last visited 10 October 2020].

Bergstrand, C. M. (1956). *Frimurarna och hundturken – vad folk trott om frimurarna*. Göteborg: Gumperts.

Best, J. (1990). *Threatened Children. Rhetoric and Concern about Child-Victims*. Chicago: University of Chicago Press.

Bibliography 107

Bjerkan, E. (2009). *Smak, omtanke og utpreget selvkritikk: Den borgerlige kvinnes mote- og skjønnhetsideal 1910–1930*. MA thesis. Department of Cultural Studies and Oriental Languages, University of Oslo.

Björkman, A. (1998). *Lies and Truths about the MV Estonia Accident*. Monaco: EGC.

Boltanski, L. (2014). *Mysteries and Conspiracies. Detective Novels and the Making of Modern Societies*. Cambridge: Polity Press.

Bomdahl, Å. (2016). Stefan Torsell söker sanningen om Estoniautredningen. *Nya Tider*. [online]. Available at: www.nyatider.nu/stefan-torsell-soker-sanningen-om-estoniakatastrofen/ [Last visited 10 November 2019].

Booth, M. (2014). *The Almost Nearly Perfect People: The Truth about the Nordic Miracle*. London: Jonathan Cabe.

Borenstein, E. (2019). *Plots Against Russia, Conspiracy and Fantasy After Socialism*. Ithaca: Cornell University Press.

Boréus, K. (2010). Including or Excluding Immigrants: The Impact of Right-Wing Populism in Denmark and Sweden, in B. Bengtsson, P. Strömblad and A-H Bay (eds.). *Diversity, Inclusion and Citizenship in Scandinavia*. Newcastle: Cambridge Scholars Publishing, pp. 127–158.

Brünnhilde. (2017). "Finnish Primary School Sex Education Book." *Save My Sweden*. 2017. www.savemysweden.com/finnish-primary-school-sex-education-book/. [Last visited 10 October 2020].

Bugge, K. L. (1927). *Det danske Frimureries Historie indtil det svenske Systems Indførelse II*. København: Rom.

Burstein, S. R. (1959). Folklore, Rumour and Prejudice. *Folklore*, 70(2), 361–381.

Butter, M. (2014). *Plots, Designs and Schemes: American Conspiracy Theories from the Puritans to the Present*. Berlin: De Gruyter.

Campion-Vincent, V. (2006). Élites Maléfiques et 'Complot Pédophile': Paniques Morales Autour Des Enfants [Evil Elites and 'Pedophile Plot': Moral Panic around Children]. *Schweizerisches Archiv Für Volkskunde*, 102, 49–70.

Carey, M. (2017). *Mistrust: An Ethnographic Theory*. Chicago: Hau Books.

Carlqvist, K. (2001). *Tysta leken – varför sjönk Estonia?* Stockholm: n/a.

Chitaladze, A., and Tughushi, N. (2018). Geworld Spreads News by Russian Troll Factory on Legalization of Necrophilia and Bestiality in Europe. *Myth Detector*. www.mythdetector.ge/en/myth/geworld-spreads-news-russian-troll-factory-legalization-necrophilia-and-bestiality-europe. [Last visited 10 October 2020].

Cohen, E., and Fennell, D. (2016). The Elimination of Marius, the Giraffe: Humanitarian Act or Callous Management Decision? *Tourism Recreation Research I*, 41(2), 168–176.

Cohn, N. (1975). *Europe's Inner Demons*. Sussex: Sussex University Press.

Crouch, D. (2016). Swedish Police Accused of Covering up Sex Attacks by Refugees at Music Festival. *The Guardian*. www.theguardian.com/world/2016/jan/11/swedish-police-accused-cover-up-sex-attacks-refugees-festival. [Last visited 10 October 2020].

Dahlstedt, M., and Neergaard, A. (2016). Crisis of Solidarity? Changing Welfare and Migration Regimes in Sweden. *Critical Sociology*, 45(1), 121–135.

Daily Worker (Dagbladet Arbejderen), www.arbejderen.dk.

108 Bibliography

Davis, S. (2005). Death in the Baltic: The M16 Connection. *New Statesman.* [online]. Available at: www.newstatesman.com/node/195304 [Last visited 14 January 2020].

DeCook, J. (2020). Coronavirus and the Radical Right: Conspiracy, Disinformation, and Xenophobia. *Open Democracy*, 13 March. www.opendemocracy.net/en/countering-radical-right/coronavirus-and-radical-right-conspiracy-disinformation-and-xenophobia/ [Last visited 27 March 2020].

De Figuiredo, I. (1994). *Nasjonal Samling 1937–1940. En analyse av partiets politiske og ideologiske utvikling fra juli 1937 til april 1940.* Oslo: Hovedoppgave i historie, Universitetet i Oslo.

Demker, M., Leffler, Y., and Sigurdson, O. (2014). Introduction: How Gloomy Is Sweden at the Millennium?, in *Culture, Health, and Religion at the Millennium. Sweden Unparadised.* New York: Palgrave Macmillan, pp. 1–18.

De Young, M. (2004). *The Day Care Ritual Abuse Moral Panic.* Jefferson, NC: McFarland.

Directorate of Health, Iceland. (2019). *Measles in Iceland.* Reykjavik: EPI-ICE, pp. 1–2.

Dyrendal, A. (2003a). *True Religions vs Cannibal Others. Rhetorical Constructions of Satanism among American Evangelicals.* Oslo: Unipub.

Dyrendal, A. (2003b). Jakten på Satans tjenere. Satanismepanikkene og den paranoide stil, in A. Pettersen and T. Emberland (eds.). *Konspiranoia. Konspirasjonsteorier fra 666 til WTC.* Oslo: Humanist forlag, pp. 229–261.

Dyrendal, A. (2011). Fusk eller heksejakt? Saken mot Eva Lundgren, in E. Balsvik and S. Solli (eds.). *Introduksjon til samfunnsvitenskapene.* Vol. 2 . Oslo: Universitetsforlaget, pp. 265–283.

Dyrendal, A. (2017). New Age and Norwegian 'Conspirituality', in I. Gilhus, S-E Kraft, and J. R. Lewis (eds.). *New Age in Norway.* Sheffield: Equinox, pp. 159–181.

Dyrendal, A. (2020). Conspiracy Beliefs about Jews and Muslims in Norway, in C. Hoffmann and V. Moe (eds.). *The Shifting Boundaries of Prejudice. Antisemitism and Islamophobia in Contemporary Norway.* Oslo: Scandinavian University Press, pp. 189–212.

Dyrendal, A., and Lap, A. O. (2008). Satanism as a News Item in Norway and Denmark. A Brief History, in J. R. Lewis and J. Petersen (eds.). *The Encyclopedic Sourcebook of Satanism.* Amherst, NY: Prometheus Books, pp. 327–360.

Ebbestad Hansen, J-E. (2018). *En antisemitt trer frem. Alf Larsen og 'Jødeproblemet'.* Oslo: Press.

Elmgren, A. (2018). 'The Jesuits of Our Time': The Jesuit Stereotype and the Year 1917 in Finland. *Journal of Jesuit Studies*, 5(1), 9–32.

Ericksson, E. (1746). *Emot Freymäurarna.* Königsberg: n/a.

Ertresvåg, P. A. (2006). *Makten bak makten.* Oslo: Koloritt.

Ertresvåg, P. A. (2008). *SOV, mitt lille Norge.* Oslo: Kolofon.

Espersen, S. (2015). DF Om Krigen Mod IS: Vi Bliver Nødt Til at Bombe Civile Nu – Også Kvinder og Børn. *TV2.* [online]. Available at: http://politik.tv2.dk/2015-11-15-df-om-krigen-mod-is-vi-bliver-noedt-til-at-bombe-civile-nu-ogsaa-kvinder-og-boern. [Last visited 3 November 2020]

Bibliography 109

Estoniasamlingen. (2019). *Estoniasamlingen.* [online]. Available at: www.estoniasamlingen.se [Last visited 10 November 2019].

European Social Survey Cumulative File, ESS 1-8 (2018). Data file edition 1.0. NSD - Norwegian Centre for Research Data, Norway - Data Archive and distributor of ESS data for ESS ERIC. doi:10.21338/NSD-ESS-CUMULATIVE.

EU vs Disinfo. (2016). Traditional European Cuisine Is under Attack of the Muslim Citizens. https://euvsdisinfo.eu/report/traditional-european-cuisine-is-under-attack-of-the-muslim-citizens/. [Last visited 10 October 2020].

EU vs Disinfo. (2017). No, Denmark Is Not Legalising Sexual Abuse of Animals. https://euvsdisinfo.eu/no-denmark-is-not-legalising-sexual-abuse-of-animals/. [Last visited 10 October 2020].

EU vs Disinfo. (2019). What Did Not Happen in 2018. https://euvsdisinfo.eu/what-did-not-happen-in-2018/. [Last visited 10 October 2020].

Evon, D. (2016a). Does a Billboard in Finland Promote Rape by Refugees? *Snopes.* www.snopes.com/fact-check/rape-billboard-finland/. [Last visited 10 October 2020].

Evon, D. (2016b). Muslim Beats Boy for Having Blue Eyes? *Snopes.* www.snopes.com/fact-check/muslim-beats-boy-for-having-blue-eyes/. [Last visited 10 October 2020].

Evon, D. (2018). Did Sweden Rename 'Christmas' to 'Winter Celebration' in Order to Avoid Offending Muslims? *Snopes.* www.snopes.com/fact-check/sweden-christmas-winter/. [Last visited 10 October 2020].

Expressen. (1995). Kända svenskar i hemlig rörelse dricker blod. *Expressen*, p. 1. [online] 23 March 2020.

Expressen. (2020). Så används coronakrisen av högerextremistiska krafter. www.expressen.se/nyheter/sa-anvands-coronakrisen-av-hogerextremistiska-krafter/ [Last visited 27 March 2020].

Fremskrittspartiets Handlingsprogram 2009–2013. (2009). [online]. Available at: www.e-pages.dk/frp/98/ [Last visited 18 April 2016].

Færseth, J. (2013). *KonspiraNorge.* Oslo: Humanist forlag.

Föreningen Vetenskap och Folkbildning. (2015). *VoF-undersökningen 2015.* Stockholm: Föreningen Vetenskap och Folkbildning.

Frykman, J. (1988). *Dansbandeländet.* Stockholm: Natur och Kultur.

Galtung, J. (2011). Ti teser om 22. juli. *Morgenbladet.* [online]. Available at: https://morgenbladet.no/samfunn/2011/ti_teser_om_22_juli [Last visited 10 November 2019].

Gashkov, I. (2018). 'Atmosfera Straha': Kak Shvetsiia Okazalas' v Zalozhnikah u Migrantov ['The Atmosphere of Fear': How Sweden Found Itself to Be a Hostage of Migrants]. *RIA Novosti.* https://ria.ru/20180112/1512452877.html [Last visited 10 October 2020].

Granrud, B. (2003). Menneskehandlere på Grev Wedels plass? Om lettlurte bønder, blaserte byfolk og beryktede frimurere, in A. Pettersen and T. Emberland (eds.). *Konspiranoia. Konspirasjonsteorier fra 666 til WTC.* Oslo: Humanist forlag, pp. 75–90.

Griffin, D. R. (2004). *The New Pearl Harbor: Disturbing Questions about the Bush Administration and 9/11.* Northampton, MA: Olive Branch Press.

110 Bibliography

Guillou, J. (2002). *Häxornas försvarare.* Stockholm: Piratförlaget.

Haaken, J. (1998). *Pillar of Salt. Gender, Memory, and the Perils of Looking Back.* New Brunswick, NJ: Rutgers University Press.

Hagelund, A. (2003). A Matter of Decency? The Progress Party in Norwegian Immigration Politics. *Journal of Ethnic and Migration Studies,* 29(1), 47–65.

Hagelund, A. (2008). For Women and Children! The Family and Immigration Politics in Scandinavia, in R. Grillo (ed.). *The Family in Question. Immigrant and Ethnic Minorities in Multicultural Europe.* Amsterdam: Amsterdam University Press, pp. 71–88.

Hansen, L. (2003). Introduction, in L. Hansen and O. Wæver (eds.). *European Integration and National Identity. The Challenge of the Nordic States.* London: Routledge, pp. 1–20.

Hansén, D., and Stern, E. (2001). From Crisis to Trauma: The Palme Assassination Case, in U. Rosenthal, R. Boin, and L. Comfort (eds.). *Managing Crises: Threats, Dilemmas, Opportunities.* Springfield, IL: Charles C. Thomas, 99. pp. 177–199.

Harrit, N. (2007). The Seventh Tower. *Information* [online]. Available at: www. information.dk/debat/2007/07/syvende-taarn.

Harrit, N. (2013). *Niels Harrit – The Seventh Tower – 911.* [video]. Available at: www.youtube.com/watch?v=PRnLmFgjPxs. [Last visited 2 November 2020]

Harrit, N. (2017). *Niels Harrit Foredrag, Det Syvende Tårn.* [video]. Available at: www.youtube.com/watch?v=kNr7t9lpTS0. [Last visited 2 November 2020]

Harrit, N. et al. (2009). Active Thermitic Material Discovered in Dust from the 9/11 World Trade Center Catastrophe. *The Open Chemical Physics Journal,* 2, 7–31.

Heinö, A. J. (2014). Sex and Sin in a Multicultural Sweden, in M. Demker, Y. Leffler, and O. Sigurdson (eds.). *Culture, Health, and Religion at the Millennium. Sweden Unparadised.* New York: Palgrave Macmillan, pp. 133–154.

Hellström, A. (2016). *Trust Us: Reproducing the Nation and the Scandinavian Nationalist Populist Parties.* New York: Berghahn Books.

Hicks, R. (1991). *In Pursuit of Satan. The Police and the Occult.* Buffalo, NY: Prometheus Books.

Hjelm, T. (2008). Driven by the Devil? Popular Constructions of Youth Satanist Careers, in J. R. Lewis and J. Petersen (eds.). *The Encyclopedic Sourcebook of Satanism.* Amherst, NY: Prometheus Books, pp. 361–380.

Hoffmann, T. (2009). Chefredaktør skrider efter kontroversiel artikel om 9/11. *Videnskab.dk* [online]. Available at: https://videnskab.dk/teknologi/chefredaktor-skrider-efter-kontroversiel-artikel-om-911. [Last visited 2 November 2020]

Holoyda, B., Sorrentino, R., Friedman, S. H., and Allgire, J. (2018). Bestiality: An Introduction for Legal and Mental Health Professionals. *Behavioral Sciences & the Law,* 36(6), 687–697.

Höjdestrand, T. (2015). Fatherland, Faith and Family Policy: Parental Mobilization against Children's Rights in Contemporary Russia. In *ICCEES IX World Congress, Makuhari, Japan.*

Höjdestrand, T. (2016). Social Welfare or Moral Warfare? *The International Journal of Children's Rights,* 24(4), 826–850.

Bibliography 111

Icelandic Review. (2016). No Money for Marrying Icelandic Maiden. www. icelandreview.com/society/no-money-marrying-icelandic-maiden/. [Last visited 10 October 2020].

Imhoff, R., and Bruder, M. (2014). Speaking (Un-)Truth to Power: Conspiracy Mentality as a Generalised Political Attitude. *European Journal of Personality*, 28, 25–43.

Jackson, K. (2015). Denmark Tells Bernie Sanders It's Had Enough Of His 'Socialist' Slurs. *Investor's Business Daily*. www.investors.com/politics/commentary/denmark-tells-bernie-sanders-to-stop-calling-it-socialist/. [Last visited 10 October 2020].

Jenkins, P. (1992). *Intimate Enemies. Moral Panics in Contemporary Great Britain*. New York: Aldine de Gruyter.

Johnson, S. (2012). Cold Case Sweden – Hunt for Killer of PM Palme Goes On. *Reuters* [online]. Available at: www.reuters.com/article/uk-sweden-palme/cold-case-sweden-hunt-for-killer-of-pm-palme-goes-on-idUKBRE83F0OE20120416 [Last visited 14 January 2020].

Jones, A. (2009). *Niels Harrit on Alex Jones Show. May 1, 2009. (part 1)*. [video]. Available at: www.youtube.com/watch?v=CfjkmTBNpD0&list=PLEAD168 BF6DA2B0A2&index=6&t=0s [Last visited 9 May, 2019].

Jones, S. E. (2006). Why Indeed Did the WTC Buildings Completely Collapse? *Journal of 9/11 Studies*, 3, 1–48.

Jupskås, A. R. (2013). The Progress Party: A Fairly Integrated Part of the Norwegian Party System, in K. Grabow and F. Hartleb (eds.). *Exposing the Demagogues: Right-Wing and National Populist Parties in Europe*. Berlin: Konrad Adenauer Stiftung, pp. 205–236.

Jupskås, A. R. (2015a). Institutionalized Right-Wing Populism in Times of Economic Crisis: A Comparative Study of the Norwegian Progress Party and the Danish People's Party, in H. Kriesi and T. S. Pappas (eds.). *European Populism in the Shadow of the Great Recession*. Colchester: ECPR Press, pp. 23–40.

Jupskås, A. R. (2015b.) The Persistence of Populism. The Norwegian Progress Party 1973–2009. [online]. Available at: www.duo.uio.no/handle/10852/48220 [Last visited 10 April 2016].

Kallestrand, G., Hahne W., Andersson P., and Ohlson J. (2015). Finland, You Do Not Want the Swedish Nightmare, *Sverigedemokratisk Ungdom*, https://debatt187.rssing.com/chan-42427119/article10.html [Last visited 2 November 2020].

Kapferer, J. N. (2013). *Rumors: Uses, Interpretations, and Images*. New Brunswick, NJ: Transaction Publishers.

Kaspak, A. (2017). Has Iceland Eliminated Down Syndrome Through Abortion? *Snopes*. www.snopes.com/fact-check/iceland-eliminated-syndrome-abortion/. [Last visited 10 October 2020].

Kasprak, A. (2018). "Is Europe Governed by 'Childless Baby Boomers'?" *Snopes*. www.snopes.com/fact-check/europe-childless-leaders/. [Last visited 10 October 2020].

Kitschelt, H., and McGann, A. (1997). *The Radical Right in Western Europe. A Comparative Analysis*. Ann Arbor, MI: University of Michigan Press.

112 Bibliography

Klein, A. (2013). The End of Solidarity? On the Development of Right-Wing Populist Parties in Denmark and Sweden, in K. Grabow and F. Hartleb (eds.). *Exposing the Demagogues: Right-Wing and National Populist Parties in Europe.* Berlin: Konrad Adenauer Stiftung, pp. 105–132.

Knight, P. (2000). *Conspiracy Culture: From Kennedy to the X-Files.* London: Routledge.

Knight, P. (2002). Introduction: A Nation of Conspiracy Theorists, in P. Knight (ed.). *Conspiracy Nation.* New York, NY: New York University Press, pp. 1–17.

Kõiv, S. (2013). Poiste Printsessipäev [A Printsess Day for Boys]. *Postimees.* https://leht.postimees.ee/1163896/poiste-printsessipaev. [Last visited 10 October 2020].

Korf, B. (2019). Breastfeeding Not Allowed? The Case of Amy J. *Step4Children Rights.* 2019. https://stepup4childrensrights.com/breastfeeding-not-allowed-the-case-of-amy-j/. [Last visited 10 October 2020].

Kosiara-Pedersen, K. (2020). 'Stronger Core, Weaker Fringes: The Danish General Election 2019'. *West European Politics,* 43(4), 1011–1022.

Kováts, E. (2017). The Emergence of Powerful Anti-Gender Movements in Europe and the Crisis of Liberal Democracy, in M. Kötti, R. Bitzan, and A. Petö (eds.). *Gender and Far Right Politics in Europe.* Basingstoke: Palgrave Macmillan, pp. 175–189.

Kringstad, H. (2007). Incest-terapi: Etter 25 år husker pasient påstått blodig drap. *Verdens Gang,* pp. 14–15.

Lacarpia, K. (2015). Dueling Memes Debate Denmark's Social Infrastructure. *Snopes.* www.snopes.com/fact-check/denmark-social-memes/ [Last visited 10 October 2020].

Lacarpia, K. (2016a). 'Offended Muslims' Attack Christmas Tree? *Snopes.* www.snopes.com/fact-check/offended-muslims-attack-christmas-tree/ [Last visited 10 October 2020].

Lacarpia, K. (2016b). Swedish Girl Refugee Assault. *Snopes.* www.snopes.com/fact-check/swedish-girl-refugee-assault-meme/ [Last visited 10 October 2020].

La Fontaine, J. S. (1998). *Speak of the Devil. Tales of Satanic Abuse in Contemporary England.* Cambridge: Cambridge University Press.

Leal, H. (2020). Networked Disinformation and the Lifecycle of Online Conspiracy Theories, in M. Butter and P. Knight (eds.). *The Routledge Handbook of Conspiracy Theories.* London: Routledge, pp. 497–511.

Leinonen, J. (2012). Invisible Immigrants, Visible Expats? *Nordic Journal of Migration Research,* 2(3), 213–223.

Lennerhed, L. (1994). *Friheten att njuta: sexualdebatten i Sverige på 1960-talet.* Stockholm: Norstedt.

Lina, J. (2004). *Architects of Deception.* Stockholm: Referent.

Ludendorff, E. (1928). *Frimureriets tillintetgörande genom avslöjandet av dess hemligheter.* Stockholm: Holmvall.

Lundgren, E. (1994). *La de små barn komme til meg. Barns erfaring med seksuelle og rituelle overgrep.* Oslo: Pax Forlag.

Bibliography 113

Lundqvist, Å., and Roman, C. (2010). The Institutionalization of Family and Gender Equality Policies in the Swedish Welfare State, in J. Fink and Å. Lundqvist (eds.). *Changing Relations of Welfare, Family, Gender and Migration in Britain and Scandinavia*, Farnham: Ashgate, pp. 65–85.

Marklund, C. (2009). Hot Love and Cold People Sexual Liberalism as Political Escapism in Radical Sweden. *NORDEUROPA Forum*, 19(1), 83–100.

Melby, K., Pylkänen, A., Rosenbeck, B., and Wetterberg, C. C. (2006). *Inte ett ord om kärlek. Äktenskap och politik i Norden ca 1850–1930*. Göteborg: Makadam Förlag.

Mikkelson, D. (2013). Blonde Extinction. *Snopes*. www.snopes.com/fact-check/gone-blonde/ [Last visited 10 October 2020].

Milne, R. (2017). Norway Minister Sparks War of Words with Sweden over Immigration. *Financial Times* [online]. Available at: www.ft.com/content/23ea67a2-8d80-11e7-a352-e46f43c5825d [Last visited 10 October 2017].

Mogstad, S. D. (1994). *Frimureriet – mysterier, felleskap, personlighetsdannelse.* Oslo: Universitetsforlaget.

Mortimore, G. (2011). Palme Conspiracy Theory Refuses to Die. *The Local*, [online]. Available at: www.thelocal.se/20110228/32306, [Last visited 10 November 2019].

Mosse, G. L. (1964). *The Crisis of German Ideology. Intellectual Origins of the Third Reich.* New York: Schocken.

Mtvuutiset.fi. (2010). *Islamin Yhdistäminen Pedofiliaan Toi Halla-Aholle Sakot Myös Hovilta. Mtv.fi.* [online]. Available at: www.mtv.fi/uutiset/rikos/artikkeli/islamin-yhdistaminen-pedofiliaan-toi-halla-aholle-sakot-myos-hovilta/2038802 [Last visited 16 February 2016].

Myhre, J. E. (2018). The Cradle of Norwegian Equality and Egalitarianism: Norway in the Nineteenth Century, in S. Bendixen, M. Bringelid, and H. Vike (eds.). *Egalitarianism in Scandinavia: Historical and Contemporary Perspectives.* London: Palgrave Macmillan, pp. 65–86.

Myrvang, C. (2003). Slemme pikers feminisme. Konsum som opprør på 1920-tallet. *Tidsskrift for ungdomsforskning*, 1(3), 67–78.

MÄN. (2018). Men, Masculinity and #MeToo: Nordic Experiences of the Movement that Shattered the Culture of Silence [online]. Available at: https://mfj.se/assets/uploads/2018/10/men-masculinity-and-metoo-web-v4.pdf. [Last visited 2 November 2020]

Nathan, D., and Snedeker, M. (1995). *Satan's Silence. Ritual Abuse and the Making of an American Witchhunt.* New York: Basic Books.

NDTV. (2012). Norway Authorities Take Away Indian Couple's Kids, Say Feeding with Hands Wrong. www.ndtv.com/india-news/norway-authorities-take-away-indian-couples-kids-say-feeding-with-hands-wrong-568169 [Last visited 10 October 2020].

Nijhuis, M. (2019). The Most Political Animal. *The Atlantic,* 27 April 2019. www.theatlantic.com/science/archive/2019/04/norway-divided-over-countrys-wolves/587302/.

NIST. (2019). FAQs – NIST's WTC 7 Investigation. *NIST* [online]. Available at: www.nist.gov/topics/disaster-failure-studies/faqs-nist-wtc-7-investigation.

114 Bibliography

Nordensvard, J., and Ketola, M. (2015). Nationalist Reframing of the Finnish and Swedish Welfare States – The Nexus of Nationalism and Social Policy in Far-Right Populist Parties. *Social Policy & Administration*, 49(3), 356–375.

Norén, A. (2019). *Mordet på statsminister Olof Palme*. [online]. Palmemordet.se Available at: www.palmemordet.se, [Last visited 10 November 2019].

Norris, P., and Inglehart, R. (2019). *Cultural Backlash. Trump, Brexit, and Authoritarian Populism*. Cambridge: Cambridge University Press.

Nyhetsmorgon. (2018). *DN har byggt en kult kring de 18 sextrakasserade kvinnorna*. [video]. Available at: www.youtube.com/watch?v=uX0ZsH3xgYI [Last visited 10 November 2019].

Oliver, J. E., and Wood, T. J. (2014). Conspiracy Theories and the Paranoid Style(s) of Mass Opinion. *American Journal of Political Science*, 58(4), 952–966.

Olmsted, K. (2010). *Real Enemies: Conspiracy Theories and American Democrazy, World War I to 9/11*. Oxford: Oxford University Press.

Palma, B. (2017). Are Police in Sweden No Longer Investigating Rapes Since Migrants Arrived? *Snopes*. www.snopes.com/fact-check/police-sweden-no-longer-investigating-since-migrants/ [Last visited 10 October 2020].

Palmemordet. (2020). [Radio Programme]. Available at: https://poddtoppen.se/podcast/1086387447/palmemordet, [Last visited 2 November 2020].

Panczová, Z. (2020). The Victims, the Guilty, and 'Us'. Notions of Victimhood in CTs in Slovakia, in A. Astapova, O. Colăcel, C. Pintilescu, and T. Scheibner (eds.). *Conspiracy Theories in Eastern Europe: Trends and Tropes*. London: Routledge, pp. 186–204.

Partiprogram. (1989). [online]. Available at: www.sdarkivet.se/files/program/program_1989.pdf [Last visited 25 May 2016].

Persson, E. (2015). Banning 'Homosexual Propaganda': Belonging and Visibility in Contemporary Russian Media. *Sexuality & Culture*, 19(2), 256–274.

Petersen, M. B., and Osmundsen, M. (2018). *Hvor udbredt er troen på konspirationsteorier i Danmark?* Working paper. Aarhus, Denmark: Institut for Statskundskab, Aarhus Universitet.

Polygraph. (2018). Fake Russian Story Stokes Anti-Immigrant Fears. *Stop Fake*. www.stopfake.org/en/fake-russian-story-stokes-anti-immigrant-fears/ [Last visited 10 October 2020].

Pullerits, P. (2018). Lastetute Võim [The Power of the Childless]. Postimees. https://arvamus.postimees.ee/6474253/priit-pullerits-lastetute-voim [Last visited 10 October 2020].

Qiu, L. (2017). Fingerprints of Russian Disinformation: From AIDS to Fake News. *New York Times*, 12 December 2017. www.nytimes.com/2017/12/12/us/politics/russian-disinformation-aids-fake-news.html [Last visited 27 March 2020].

Rabo, A. (2009). Den goda familjen och den goda familjerätten. Debatter om lag och moral i det mångkulturella Europa, *Socialvetenskaplig Tidskrift*, 16(3–4), 300–319.

Raunio, T. (2013). The Finns: Filling a Cap in the Party System, in K. Grabow and F. Hartleb (eds.). *Exposing the Demagogues: Right-Wing and National Populist Parties in Europe*. Berlin: Konrad Adenauer Stiftung, pp. 133–160.

Bibliography 115

Ravn, A. B., and Rosenbeck, B. (2010). Competing Meanings of Gender Equality. Family, Marriage and Tax Laws in 20th Century Denmark, in J. Fink and Å. Lundqvist (eds.). *Changing Relations of Welfare, Family, Gender and Migration in Britain and Scandinavia.* Farnham: Ashgate. pp. 39–63.

Renz, B. (2016). Russia and 'Hybrid Warfare.' *Contemporary Politics,* 22(3), 283–300.

Ringberg, J., and Lerche Kristiansen, A. (2019). Historien om Stram Kurs: YouTube-fænomenet, der pludselig fik medvind og kom på stemmesedlen, *dr.dk,* www.dr.dk/nyheder/webfeature/stram-kurs [Last visited 3 November 2020]

Roach, M. (2013). Let's Talk About the Orgasm. *Huffpost.* www.huffingtonpost. com/mary-roach/orgasm-ted-talk_b_2689995.html [Last visited 3 November 2020]

Robbins, B. (2017). The Detective Is Suspended: Nordic Noir and the Welfare State, in L. Nilsson, D. Damrosch, and T. Dhaen (eds.). *Crime Fiction as World Literature.* London: Bloomsbury Academic, pp. 47–58.

Rosenberg, G. (2002). The Crisis of Consensus in Postwar Sweden, in N. Witoszek and L. Trägårdh (eds.). *Culture and Crisis. The Case of Germany and Sweden.* New York and Oxford: Berghahn Books, pp. 170–201.

Rosenthal, U., Boin, A., and Comfort, L. K. (2001). *Managing Crises: Threats, Dilemmas, Opportunities.* Springfield, IL: Charles C. Thomas, pp. 177–199.

Rudstrøm, E. (2005). *Frimureriet og de skjulte makteliter I and II.* Oslo: Norelco.

Ruth, A. (1995). Det Moderna Sveriges Myter, in B. Linell and M. Löfgren (eds.). *Svenska Krusbär. En Historiebok Om Sverige Och Svenskar.* Stockholm: Bonnier Alba, pp. 544–571.

Rydgren, J. (2007). The Sociology of the Radical Right. *Annual Review of Sociology,* 33, 241–262.

Rytter, M. (2010). 'The Family of Denmark' and 'the Aliens'. Kinship Images in Danish Integration Politics. *Ethnos,* 75(3), 301–322.

Salonen, R. (2019). "Na Zapade Idet Neob'iavlennaia Ohota Na Russkih Detei." File RF. http://file-rf.ru/news/6697. [Last visited 10 October 2020].

Schlink, M. B. (1976). *Patmos – da himmelen åpnet seg.* Oslo: Luther forlag.

Seierstad, Å. (2015). *One of Us: The Story of Anders Breivik and the Massacre in Norway.* 1st edition. New York: Farrar, Straus and Giroux.

Simonnes, K. (2011). I Stjålne klær? *En Analyse Av Endringer i Høyres, Arbeiderpartiets Og Fremskrittspartiets Innvandrings-Og Integreringspolitikk Fra 1985 Til 2009.* MA thesis. Universitetet i Oslo.

Simonsen, K. B. (2019). Holocaustbenektelse i Folk og Land (8.mai) 1948–1975. En diskurs tar form. *Historisk Tidsskrift,* 1, 8–25.

Skaf, M. (2012). Novaia Detskaia Literaratura [New Children's Literature]. Oktiabr'. https://magazines.gorky.media/october/2012/12/novaya-detskaya-literatura.html. [Last visited 10 October 2020].

Skarsgård, K. (2019). Genusforskningen i skottgluggen. *Universitetsläraren,* nr. 3, 23–29.

Skarvoy, L., and Svendsen, S. (2011). Dansk Partileder Refser Siv Jensen: – Hun Mangler Ryggrad. *VG.* [online]. Available at: www.vg.no/nyheter/innenriks/22-juli/artikkel.php?artid=10089142 [Last visited 20 April 2016].

116 Bibliography

Smallpage, S. M., Drochon, H., Uscinski, J. E., and Klofstad, C. (2020). Who Are the Conspiracy Theorists? The Problems of Comparing Demographics and Conspiracy Theories, in M. Butter and P. Knight (eds.). *Handbook of Conspiracy Theories*. London: Routledge. pp. 263–277.

Sommer, N., and Aagaard, S. (2003). *Succes: Historien Om Pia Kjærsgaard*. Lindhardt og Ringhof.

Sontag, S. (1969). A Letter from Sweden. Ramparts Magazine July 1969, 23–38. [online] https://www.unz.com/print/Ramparts-1969jul-00023/ [last visited 2 November 2020]

Sparks, I. (2014). Denmark to Finally Ban Animal Sex Because It's 'Damaging the Country's Reputation.' *Express*. www.express.co.uk/news/world/522293/Animal-Sex-Beastiality-Reputation-Country-Denmark. [Last visited 10 October 2020].

Stidsen, M. (2018). Vänsterpopulistisk revolution revolt hotar Svenska Akademien. *Expressen*. [online]. Available at: www.expressen.se/kultur/ide/vansterpopulistisk-revolt-hotar-svenska-akademien/ [Last visited 10 November 2019].

Stougaard-Nielsen, J. (2016). Nordic Noir in the UK: The Allure of Accessible Difference. *Journal of Aesthetics & Culture*, 8(1), DOI: 10.3402/jac.v8.32704 [Last visited 27 March 2020].

Sundell, N., Dotevall, L., Sansone, M., Andersson, M., Lindh, M., Wahlberg, T., Tyrberg, T., Westin, J., Liljeqvist, J., Bergström, T., and Studahl, M. (2019). Measles Outbreak in Gothenburg Urban Area, Sweden, 2017 to 2018: Low Viral Load in Breakthrough Infections. *Eurosurveillance*, 24(17), 1–11.

Sundhedsstyrelsen. (2019). Børnevaccinationsprogrammet – Årsrapport 2018. [online]. Available at: www.sst.dk/da/nyheder/2019/~/media/02CBB557937E4218AE5F742CA642FA9B.ashx [Last visited 3 November 2020]

Sveland, M. (2013). *Hatet. En bok om antifeminism*. Stockholm: Leopard förlag/Pocketförlaget.

Svenska Palmen. (2012). Sotsial'naia Zaschita Otniala Rebenka. *Sweden4Rus*. http://sweden4rus.nu/forum/viewmsg?page=56&pid=11670 [Last visited 3 November 2020]

Sverigedemokraternas Principprogram. (2003). [online], https://snd.gu.se/sv/vivill/party/sd/p/2003 [Last visited 2 November 2020]

Szyma, K. (2018). The Eristic of Newsworthiness in the Representation of Barnevernet Controversy: A Case Study of the Norwegian Child Welfare Service. *Retoryka Dziennikarstwa Rhetoric of / in Journalism*, 5(1), 1–20.

Sæland, I. (2016). Facebook Post. Inga Sæland.

Thalmann, K. (2014). 'John Birch Blues': The Problematization of Conspiracy Theory in the Early Cold War. *COPAS*, 15(1), 1–17.

Thalmann, K. (2019). *The Stigmatization of Conspiracy Theory Since the 1950's*. London: Routledge.

The Local. (2013). Norway Wants Brazil Kid in Care 'for Eating Wrong.' www.thelocal.no/20131204/norway-fights-to-take-brazilian-child-into-care-for-eating-wrong. [Last visited 3 November 2020]

The Local. (2015a). Norway Care System 'like Nazis': Czech President. [online] www.thelocal.no/20150210/norways-foster-care-system-like-nazi-programme. [Last visited 10 October 2020]

Bibliography 117

The Local. (2015b). 'Norway Took My Child Because of Pretty Dress.' [online] www.thelocal.no/20150828/norway-accused-of-taking-immigrant-children. [Last visited 10 October 2020]

The Local. (2017). Meeting between Swedish and Norwegian Ministers Scrapped Following 'No-Go Zone' Claims. *The Local.* [online]. www.thelocal. no/20170829/meeting-between-swedish-and-norwegian-ministers-scrapped-following-no-go-zone-claims [Last visited 19 October 2017].

Thomas, D. (2011). The 9/11 Truth Movement: The Top Conspiracy Theory, a Decade Later. *Skeptical Inquirer*, 35(4). https://skepticalinquirer.org/2011/07/the-911-truth-movement-the-top-conspiracy-theory-a-decade-later/. [Last visited 10 October 2020]

Thórisdóttir, H. (forthcoming). Social Engagement and Conspiracy Beliefs.

Thrana, H. M., and Fauske, H. (2014). The Emotional Encounter with Child Welfare Services : The Importance of Incorporating the Emotional Perspective in Parents' Encounters with Child Welfare Workers. *European Journal of Social Work*, 17(2), 221–236.

Topping, A. (2017). 'Sweden, Who Would Believe This?': Trump Cites Non-Existent Terror Attack. *The Guardian.* www.theguardian.com/us-news/2017/feb/19/sweden-trump-cites-non-existent-terror-attack. [Last visited 10 October 2020]

Torsell, S. (2016). *M/S Estonia – Svenska statens haveri.* Stockholm: AlternaMedia.

Trykkefrihedsselskabet. (2019). *Video: Er Sverige tabt?.* [video]. Available at: www.trykkefrihed.dk/video-er-sverige-tabt.htm, [Last visited 10 November 2019].

Tunander, O. (2011). Inspiratorer, interessenter, innvielsesmestre og investorer i Breiviks verden. *Nytt Norsk Tidskrift*, 4, 348–358.

Ullgren, P. (2010). *Hemligheternas brödraskap: om de svenska frimurarna.* Stockholm: Norstedts.

Ulvund, F. (2017). *Nasjonens antiborgere.Forestillinger om religiøse minoriteter som samfunnsfiender i Norge, ca. 1814–1964.* Oslo: CappelenDamm.

Uscinski, J. E., and Parent, J. M. (2014). *American Conspiracy Theories.* New York, NY: Oxford University Press.

van Prooijen, J.-W. (2019). Empowerment as a Tool to Reduce Belief in Conspiracy Theories, in U. Joe (ed.). *Conspiracy Theories and the People Who Believe Them.* New York: Oxford University Press, pp. 432–442.

van Prooijen, J.-W., Krouwel, A. P. M., and Pollet, T. V. (2015). Political extremism predicts belief in conspiracy theories. *Social Psychological and Personality Science*, 6, 570–578.

Varnava, F. (2016). V Shvetsii Zapretili Rozhdestvenskie Ogni [Christmas Lights Are Illegal in Sweden]. http://barnabasfund.ru/ru/v-shvetsii-zapretili-rozhdestvenskie-ogni/. [Last visited 10 October 2020]

Victor, J. S. (1990). Satanic Cult Rumors as Contemporary Legend. *Western Folklore*, 49(1), 51–81.

Victor, J. S. (1993). *Satanic Panic. The Making of a Contemporary Legend.* Chicago: Open Court.

Victor, J. S. (1998). Moral Panics and the Social Construction of Deviant Behavior: A Theory and Application to the Case of Ritual Child Abuse. *Sociological Perspectives*, 41(3), 541–565.

118 *Bibliography*

Villemoes, S. K. (2012). Galskab i Den Sorte Diamant. *Weekendavisen*.

Viral. (2017). Farewell, My Friend! Danish Zoos Accept Pets as Predator Feed. *Sputnik News*. https://sputniknews.com/viral/201712221060228105-denmark-pets-animal-cruelty/. [Last visited 10 October 2020]

Visegrad Post. (2018). Polish Parliamentarians Met Silje Garmo, the Norwegian Woman Who Asked for Asylum in Poland for Fleeing Barnevernet with Her Daughter. https://visegradpost.com/en/2018/06/19/polish-parliamentarians-met-silje-garmo-the-norwegian-woman-who-asked-for-asylum-in-poland-for-fleeing-barnevernet-with-her-daughter/. [Last visited 10 October 2020]

Watson, A. (2013). 12 'Myths' about Education in Finland Debunked. *The Cornerstone for Teachers*. https://thecornerstoneforteachers.com/12-myths-about-education-in-finland-debunked/. [Last visited 10 October 2020]

Wellcome Trust. (2019). *Wellcome Global Monitor 2018*. [online]. Available at: https://wellcome.ac.uk/reports/wellcome-global-monitor/2018 [Last visited 16 January 2020].

West-Knights, I. (2019). Who Killed the Prime Minister? The Unsolved Murder That Still Haunts Sweden. *The Guardian*. [online]. Available at: www.theguardian.com/news/2019/may/16/olof-palme-sweden-prime-minister-unsolved-murder-new-evidence, [Last visited 10 November 2019].

Widfeldt, A. (2015). *Extreme Right Parties in Scandinavia*. New York: Routledge.

Winneker, C. (2015). Finnish Politician Declares War on 'Multiculturalism'. *Politico*. [online]. Available at: www.politico.eu/article/finland-immonen-stubb-immigration-multiculturalism/ [Last visited 16 February 2016].

Witte, H. (1999). *M/S Estonia sänktes. Nya fakta och teorier*. Stockholm: Witte.

Wong, O. (2018). Ansvaret för akademidrevet faller tungt på Björn Wiman'. *Svenska Dagbladet*. [online]. Available at: www.svd.se/ansvaret-for-akademidrevet-faller-tungt-pa-bjorn-wiman, [Last visited 10 November 2019].

Wren, K. (2001). Cultural Racism: Something Rotten in the State of Denmark? *Social & Cultural Geography*, 2(2), 141–162.

Yle.fi. (2008). *Police to Investigate Helsinki City Council Member's Blog*. *Yle Uutiset*. [online]. Available at: http://yle.fi/uutiset/police_to_investigate_helsinki_city_council_members_blog/6127584 [Last visited 16 February 2016].

Zuquete, J. P. (2018). *The Identitarians. The Movement against Globalism and Islam in Europe*. Notre Dame, IN: University of Notre Dame Press.

Önnerfors, A. (2003). *Svenska Pommen – kultumöten och identifikation*. Lund: Minerva.

Önnerfors, A. (2017a). Between Breivik and PEGIDA: The Absence of Ideologues and Leaders in the Contemporary European Far-Right. *Patterns of Prejudice*, 51(2), 159–175.

Önnerfors, A. (2017b). *Freemasonry – A Very Short Introduction*. Oxford: OUP.

Önnerfors, A. (2018). Pride against Prejudice: Swedish Superhero Episode Strikes Against the Radical Right. *Centre for Analysis of the Radical Rights*. [online]. Available at: www.radicalrightanalysis.com/2018/09/04/pride-against-prejudice-swedish-superhero-episode-strikes-against-the-radical-right/ [Last visited 4 September 2018].

Bibliography 119

Önnerfors, A. (forthcoming). Fraternal Kingdom? Freemasonry at the Court of Gustav III of Sweden (1772–1792), in T. Biskup (ed.). *Enlightenment at Court*. Oxford: Voltaire Foundation.

Önnerfors, A. (2020). Criminal Cosmopolitans: Conspiracy Theories Surrounding the Assassination of Gustav III of Sweden in 1792, in T. Haug and A. J. Krischer (eds.). *Höllische Ingenieure: Attentate und Verschwörungen in kriminalitäts-, entscheidungs- und sicheheitsgeschichtlicher Pespektive.* Konstanz: Universitätsverlag Konstanz. 137–151

Østbye, H. N. (1941). *Jødenes krig.* Oslo: Kamban forlag.

Åkesson, J. (2009a). Min avsikt har aldrig varit att såra någon. *Mynewsdesk.* [online]. Available at: www.mynewsdesk.com/se/sverigedemokraterna/pressreleases/min-avsikt-har-aldrig-varit-att-saara-naagon-jimmie-aakesson-kommenterar-kalibers-senaste-saendning-285006 [Last visited 10 November 2019].

Åkesson, J. (2009b). Muslimerna Är Vårt Största Utländska Hot. *Aftonbladet.* [online]. Available at: www.aftonbladet.se/debatt/debattamnen/politik/article12049791.ab [Last visited 27 May 2016].

Åsard, E. (2006). *Det dunkelt tänkta: konspirationsteorier om morden på John F Kennedy och Olof Palme.* Stockholm: Ordfront.

DI: Democracy Index. www.eiu.com/topic/democracy-index.
GGG: Global Gender Gap www3.weforum.org/docs/WEF_GGGR_2018.pdf.
GPI: Global Peace Index. http://visionofhumanity.org.
HDI: Human development index. http://hdr.undp.org/en/composite/HDI.

Index

Andersson, Lena, 50
anti-feminist conspiracy theories, 49–51, 95–96
anti-globalization conspiracy theories, 3, 12, 94
anti-immigrant conspiracy theories, 12, 56–58, 63–65, 89, 91, 101; Breivik's manifesto, 19, 49, 51, 53; in Denmark, 61–63; Eurabia theory, 13, 53, 57–58, 62–64, 72; fake news in Sweden, 82–85; in Finland, 58, 66–68; in Iceland, 69; in Norway, 57–60; in Sweden, 70–72, 83. *See also* conspiracy theories in Nordic countries; migration; Muslim migrant conspiracy theories
anti-Semitism, 12, 18–20, 39–42, 90, 99; early, 54–56; Holocaust deniers and, 29, 42
antifa, 95
Arnault, Jean-Claude, 50–51
Åsard, E., 21, 24
authoritarianism, 3
Åkesson, Jimmie, 71–72

Barkun, M., 93
Barnevernet stories, 76–81, 86, 88
Bergseth, Irina, 75–78
bestiality in Denmark, 13, 85–88
Björkman, Anders, 23–24
Boltanski, Luc, 99
Breivik, Anders Behring, 12–13, 19–20, 49, 51, 53, 63–65, 96, 98

Camre, Mogens, 58
Camus, Renaud, 53
cannibalism, 33–37, 45
Carlqvist, Knut, 23
chemtrail conspiracy theories, 16
climate change conspiracy theories, 24, 92, 95, 101–2
Cohn, Norman, 34
conspiracy theories (general): abundance of claims after significant events and, 19; deep state conspiracy theories, 12, 20–22, 26, 31; defined, 4; extremism and, 54; international travel of, 3, 9, 18, 90; low social trust and, 4–5, 101; moon-landing conspiracy theories, 10; as rarely repeating exactly but frequently rhyming, 34, 103; as resilient and evolving, 89; as symptom of underlying anger and/or anxiety, 4, 13; as theodicy, 3, 45, 102; UFOs and, 25–26; United States as global centre of, 9, 12, 16, 90, 94; vaccine conspiracy theories, 10–11, **11**, 16, 31, 93–94
conspiracy theories (U.S.), 102; deep state conspiracy theories, 12, 20–22, 26, 31; moon-landing conspiracy theories, 10; Satanic, 45; U.S. as epicenter of, 9, 12, 16, 90, 94; vaccines and vaccine conspiracy theories, 10–11, **11**. *See also* 9/11-related conspiracy theories

122 *Index*

conspiracy theories *about* Nordic countries, 4, 13, 73–75, 95; *Barnevernet* (Norwegian Child Welfare Services) and, 76–81, 85–86, 88; bestiality in Denmark and, 13, 85–86; fake news in Sweden, 82–85; of Nordic family and children, 77–82; of Nordic sexual amorality, 75–77

conspiracy theories in Nordic countries, 91, 103; 9/11-related conspiracy theories and, 8–10, 16, 25–31, 58, 92; assassination of King Gustav III (Sweden) and, 12, 16, 18; English language proficiency and American narratives, 9, 16, 90, 94; *Estonia* ferry sinking in 1994 and, 2, 12, 15, 23–25; as exogenous impacts and cultural globalization, 15–16, 90, 92; financial crisis-related in Iceland, 2–3, 68–69, 91–92; gender equality as specifically Nordic trait and, 43–44; health and disease conspiracy theories, 92–93; Iceland as highest prevalence of and political trust levels of, 11; increase of in last 50 years, 3; international travel of, 9, 93; lack of exceptionalism for, 13; media coverage of, 102; moon-landing conspiracy theories and, 10; murder of Olaf Palme (Swedish P.M.) and, 1–2, 12, 15, 21–23, 89; Nordic noir crime novels and, 99–101; Nordic perception of belonging to 'irrational other' and, 4; ritual murder and cannibalism conspiracy (1869, Norway), 33–37; as symptom of underlying anger and/or anxiety, 13; underdeveloped field of study of, 3, 9; vaccine conspiracy theories, 10–11, **11**, 16, 31, 93–94; wolf pack conspiracy theories and, 91–92. *See also* 9/11-related conspiracy theories; anti-immigrant conspiracy theories; family, gender and sexuality conspiracy lore in Nordic

countries; Nordic populist right-wing conspiracy theories

Covid-19, 93–94, 98

crime novels, 1. *See also* Nordic noir

cultural diffusion of conspiracy narratives, 3–4

cultural Marxism, 49–51, 53, 81, 97–98

cultural Nordism, 7–8

cultural racism, 56, 60

deep state conspiracy theories, 12, 15, 20, 22, 26, 31; murder of Olof Palme and, 21

Denmark: 9/11 related conspiracy theories and, 9, 58; bestiality conspiracy theories, 13, 85–86; Freemasonry and elite sociability in, 15, 17, 19; gender equality, 59; migrants and migration in, 56–57; money laundering scandals in, 8; Muslim migrant conspiracy theories in, 58–59, 61–63; state formation in, 15; vaccines and vaccine conspiracy theories, 10–11, **11**. *See also* 9/11-related conspiracy theories (Nordic countries); Nordic states

Disaster of the Swedish State (Torsell), 24

elites and secret societies conspiracy theories, 3, 8, 89, 91, 94, 101; 9/11-related conspiracy theories and, 25–31; deep state conspiracy theories, 12, 15, 20–22, 26, 31; EU policies and, 66, 69, 72; Eurabian conspiracy theories and, 53, 57, 64; financial crisis and, 8; forgotten people in Finland and, 66–67; Jewish-Masonic world conspiracy and, 18–21; secret societies and, 16–19; sexual themed conspiracy theories and, 41–42, 45. *See also* Freemasonry; Satanic conspiracy theories

English language proficiency, 9, 90; increase in conspiracy narratives and, 3

Ertresvåg, Per-Aslak, 20

Index 123

Estonia sinking conspiracy theories (1994), 2, 12, 15, 23–25
Eurabia theory, 13, 53, 57–58, 62–64, 72. *See also* anti-immigrant conspiracy theories; Breivik, Anders Behring
European Social Survey (ESS), 6–7
European Union (EU), 8, 61, 72; energy legislation, 69, 92; EU bailouts, 66; Eurabia theory and Great Replacement theory and, 53, 57–58; Nordic countries and, 7
extremism, 53–55, 61–63, 65–68, 70–72

fake news, 75, 80, 82–86, 88, 93
family, gender and sexuality conspiracy lore in Nordic countries, 52, 95, 97–98, 101; *about* Nordic family and children, 77–82, 85–88; *about* Nordic sexual amorality, 75–77; anti-feminist conspiracy theories, 49–51, 95–96; anti-Semitism and Nordic Nazi's and, 39–41; *Barnevernet* (Norwegian Child Welfare Services) and, 76–81, 85–86, 88; bestiality fake news in Denmark and, 85–86; Covid-19 and, 93–94, 98; fake news in Sweden, 82–85; family punishment criminalization and, 44; family reforms, 12–13, 34–35, 38; gender equality, 5, 43–44, 59, 96; gender equality as specifically Nordic trait and, 43–44; HIV/AIDS conspiracy theories, 90; homosexuality, 40–43, 75–76, 80–81, 97; identity politics and, 49–50; Incel culture and, 96; international origins and Outsider discourses of, 52; #MeToo movement, 50; nationalism and women's rights emergence and, 35; Nordic Nazi and sexual morality conspiracy theories, 39–41; Nordic noir crime novels and, 99; in postwar period, 41–43; problematic youth culture of 1930s and 1940s and, 38; repeating themes of

concern and demonization in, 34; ritual murder and cannibalism conspiracy and, 35–37; Satanic conspiracy theories and, 33–34, 44–49; sexuality in Sweden *vs.* Norway, 75; Södertälje case (Sweden) and feminism, 33–34; sterilization programmes and social engineering, 37
ferry sinking *(Estonia,* 1994), 2, 12, 15, 23–25
financial crisis, 8, 66; conspiracy theory in Iceland, 2–3, 68–69, 91–92
Finland, 13; anti-immigration and xenophobia in, 58, 66–68; as conspiracy conduit to Russia, 90; Freemasonry in, 18–19; migrants and migration in, 58; vaccines and vaccine relates conspiracy theories, 11, **11**; wolf pack conspiracy theories and, 91–92. *See also* conspiracy theories in Nordic countries; Nordic states
Five (5)G-net conspiracy theories, 16, 94
France: high trust in national parliaments of *vs.* in Nordic and other Euro countries, 6, *6*; social trust in, 7, *7*; social trust in *vs.* other Nordic and other Euro states, 7, *7*; vaccines and vaccine conspiracy theories, 11
Freemasonry, 15–19, 94; Anders Behring Breivik terror attacks and, 19–20; in Denmark, 17, 19; in Finland, 18–19; in Norway, 19–20; Satanism and, 17, 19, 36; in Sweden, 15–19. *See also* Knights Templar; secret societies
Frich, Øvre Richter, 99
Frostensson, Katarina, 50

Galtung, Johan, 19–20
Gates, Bill, 93, 95
gender equality, 5, 43–44, 59, 96; as specifically Nordic trait, 43–44. *See also* family, gender and sexuality conspiracy lore in Nordic countries

124   *Index*

Germany, 6–8, *6–7*; vaccines and vaccine conspiracy theories, 11

Glistrup, Mogens, 58

Great Replacement Theory, 53, 72

Great Replacement, The (Camus), 53

Gunnlaugsson, Sigmunddur (Prime Minister of Iceland), 3, 69, 92

Harrit, 26–28

HIV/AIDS conspiracy theories, 90

Holocaust denial, 29, 42

homosexuality, 40, 43, 75–76, 80–81, 97; in post-war conspiracy, 41–42. *See also* family, gender and sexuality conspiracy lore in Nordic countries

human rights, 12

Iceland, 13; 9/11-related conspiracy theories in, 9–10; financial crisis-related conspiracy theories and, 2–3, 68–69, 91–92; as Nordic country with highest prevalence of conspiracy theories and lowest political trust, 11; populism and anti-Muslim rhetoric in, 68–69; vaccines and vaccine conspiracy theories, 10–11, **11**. *See also* 9/11-related conspiracy theories (Nordic countries); Nordic states

identity politics, 49–50

Jensen, Siv, 63–64

Jewish-Masonic world conspiracy, 18–21

King Gustav III (Sweden), 12, 16, 18

Kjærsgaard, Pia, 58, 61

Knights Templar, 12, 17, 19–20

Lange, Anders, 57

Larsson, Steig, 2

LGBTQ movement and community, 44, 65, 76, 78, 81. *See also* family, gender and sexuality conspiracy lore in Nordic countries

Lina, Jüri, 19, 23

Listhaug, Sylvi, 65–66

Ludendorff, Erich, 18

Mankell, Henning, 2

marriage: as gender-neutral in Nordic countries, 44

masculinity, 49, 52, 97

media coverage, 102

migrants and migration, 3, 12–13, 56; economic downturn and, 8; fake news in Sweden, 82–85; fear of, 72; in Finland, 58; in Norway, 59; post-war, 43; Trump's fake news speech on European, 82. *See also* anti-immigrant conspiracy theories; Muslim migrant conspiracy theories

Mogstad, Sverre Dag, 19

moon-landing (U.S., 1969) conspiracy theories, 10

murder of Olof Palme (Swedish P.M.), 1–2, 12, 15, 21–23, 89; as collective trauma and influence on Nordic Noir, 2

murder, ritual, 33–37

Muslim migrant conspiracy theories, 53, 67, 71–72, 82, 84, 86, 95; in Denmark, 57–59, 61–63; in Finland, 67–68; in Iceland, 68–69; in Norway, 57–58, 60–61, 63–65; in Sweden, 72, 83. *See also* anti-immigrant conspiracy theories

Muslims, 13; Eurabia theory and, 53. *See also* Eurabia theory

Neutzsky-Wulff, Erwin, 45

9/11-related conspiracy theories, 9–10, 16, 25–31, 92; Denmark and, 58; war on terror and, 8

Nobel Prize, 50–51

Nordic countries, 5; cultural Nordism of, 7–8; European Union (EU) membership and, 7; gender equality as specifically Nordic trait in, 43–44; high trust in national parliaments in, 6, *6*; identity politics in, 49–50; intra-inclusiveness of, 8; marriage in, 44; migration and economic downturn and, 8; Norden concept and European project participation, 7–8; positive international image and ranking of, 5, **6**, 34, 73–74;

Index 125

snapshot of, 5; social engineering in, 37; social trust in Nordic *vs.* other Euro states, 7, *7*; state formation in, 15, 55; xenophobia in, 8, 60, 66–68, 70, 72–73. *See also* Denmark; Finland; Iceland; Norway; Sweden
Nordic exceptionalism, 13, 49, 101–3
Nordic Nazi conspiracy theories, 39–41
Nordic noir, 89, 99–100; murder of Prime Minister Palme and, 1–2
Nordic populist right-wing conspiracy theories, 54, 72; in Denmark, 56–59, 61–63; in Finland, 58, 66–68; in Iceland, 68–69; in Norway, 57–58, 63–66; in Sweden, 70–72. *See also* Eurabia theory; Great Replacement Theory
Norway: anti-immigration in, 57–60; *Barnevernet* (Norwegian Child Welfare Services) of, 76–81, 85–86, 88; Covid-19 conspiracies, 93–94, 98; family and sexual norms conspiracy theories, 13; far-right extremism and racism in, 57–59, 64–66; Freemasonry in, 19–20; Muslim migrant conspiracy theories in, 57–61, 65; ritual murder and cannibalism conspiracy (1869), 35–37; sexuality in *vs.* Sweden, 75; terrorist attacks of in 2011, 12–13, 15, 19–20, 53; vaccines and vaccine relates conspiracy theories, 11, **11**; wolf pack conspiracy theories and, 91–92. *See also* Breivik, Anders Behring; conspiracy theories in Nordic countries; Nordic states
Novel of a Crime (Wahlöö), 99

oil crisis (1972), 12
Østbye, H.N., 39–40, 51
others. *See* outsiders discourse and theories
Ouija boards, 45
outsiders discourse and theories, 8, 12, 24, 49, 51–54, 89, 91, 95; dehumanization and exclusionary politics and, 72; in Denmark,

56–57; in Nordic noir (Nordic crime novels), 98–101. *See also* anti-immigrant conspiracy theories; anti-Semitism; Muslim migrant conspiracy theories

Palme, Olof (Swedish Prime Minister), 1–2, 12, 15, 21–23. *See also* murder of Olof Palme (Swedish P.M.)
Parent, J.M., 4, 102
Parliament: high trust in national parliaments in Nordic *vs.* other Euro countries, 6, *6*
Pettersson, Christer, 21
Poland, 8, 81
political trust: in Iceland, 11
popular culture, 45, 48; U.S. and spread of U.S. conspiracy theories, 9, 90
populism, 3, 53, 57, 59, 62, 66, 68–70, 72
Protocols of the Elders of Zion, 18–20, 90

ritual murder and cannibalism conspiracy (1869, Norway), 35–37
Rudstrøm, Erik, 20
Russia, 93; conspiracy theories *about* Nordic countries and, 4, 75–78; *Estonia* sinking and, 23–24; Finland as conspiracy conduit to, 90; *Protocol of the Elders of Zion* and Jewish-Masonic conspiracies, 18

Satanic conspiracy theories, 43–49; Freemasonry and, 17, 19, 36; in Sweden, 33–34
secret societies, 16–19, 94. *See also* Freemasonry
sexuality, 40–43, 52; bestiality fake news in Denmark and, 85–86; conspiracy theories *about* Nordic sexual amorality, 75–77; HIV/AIDS conspiracy theories, 90; homosexuality, 40–43, 75–76, 80–81, 97; Incel culture and, 96; LGBTQ movement and community, 44, 65, 76, 78, 81; in

126　*Index*

Norway *vs.* Sweden, 74–75. *See also*
family, gender and sexuality
conspiracy lore in Nordic countries
Sjöwall, Maj, 99
social engineering, 37
social liberalism, 3
social trust, 101; conspiracy beliefs
and, 5; higher levels in Nordic *vs.*
other Euro states, 7, *7*
Södertälje case (Sweden), 33–34
Soini, Timo, 66–68
Sontag, Susan, 74
state based conspiracy theories,
3, 8, 12; *Estonia* ferry sinking
and, 23–25; Olof Plame murder
and, 21–23. *See also* 9/11-related
conspiracy theories; *Estonia*
sinking conspiracy theories
(1994); murder of Olof Palme
(Swedish P.M.)
sterilization programmes, 37
Stidsen, Marianne, 50–51
stigmatized knowledge claims, 93
Sweden: 9/11 related conspiracy
theories and, 9; anti-immigrant
conspiracy theories in, 70–72, 83;
assassination of King Gustav III
(Sweden) and, 12, 16, 18; *Estonia*
ferry sinking and, 23–25; fake
news in, 82–85; Freemasonry and
secret societies in, 15–19; migrants
and migration in, 13, 56; money
laundering scandals in, 8; murder
of Olaf Palme (Swedish P.M.)
and, 21–23; Satanism in, 33–34;
sexuality in *vs.* Norway, 75; state
formation in, 15; vaccines and
vaccine relates conspiracy theories,
10–11, **11**; welfare paradise

narrative of, 73–75; wolf pack
conspiracy theories and, 91–92.
See also 9/11-related conspiracy
theories (Nordic countries);
conspiracy theories in Nordic
countries; murder of Olof Palme;
Nordic states

theodicy, 3, 45, 102
Thunberg, Greta, 95–96
Torsell, Stefan, 23
trauma theories, 21–31
Trump, Donald, 82
Truther movement, 25–31. *See also*
9/11-related conspiracy theories
Tunander, Ola, 19–20

UFOs, 25–26
United States. *See* conspiracy
theories (U.S.)
Uscinski, J.E., 4, 102

vaccine conspiracy theories, 10–11,
11, 16, 31, 93–94
von Höpken, Anders, 16

Wahlöö, Per, 99
Wakefield, Andrew, 10
war on terror, 8, 16
welfare, 8, 41, 73–74; Nordic noir
crime novels and, 99–100; welfare
chauvinism, 67, 69, 71–72; welfare
paradise narrative, 3, 73–75
wolf pack conspiracy theories,
91–92
Wren, Karen, 56

xenophobia, 60, 66–68, 70, 72–73;
economic downturn and, 8